THE
OPEN
WINDOW

8 WEEKS TO CREATING
AN EXTRAORDINARY LIFE

Catherine Galasso-Vigorito

TURNER

Turner Publishing Company
200 4th Avenue North • Suite 950 Nashville, Tennessee 37219
445 Park Avenue • 9th Floor New York, NY 10022

www.turnerpublishing.com

The Open Window: 8 Weeks to Creating an Extraordinary Life

All Scripture references and quotations from this book are used from the King James Version (KJV) unless otherwise noted.

Other references are from the following:

Amplified Bible (AMP) Copyright © 1954, 1958, 1962, 1964, 1965, 1987 by The Lockman Foundation.

Contemporary English Version (CEV) Copyright © 1995 by American Bible Society.

The Holy Bible, English Standard Version (ESV) Copyright © 2001 by Crossway Bibles, a division of Good News Publishers.

Good News Translation (GNT) Copyright © 1992 by American Bible Society.

Holman Christian Standard Bible (HCSB) Copyright © 1999, 2000, 2002, 2003 by Holman Bible Publishers, Nashville Tennessee. All rights reserved.

New American Standard Bible (NASB) Copyright © 1960, 1962, 1963, 1968, 1971, 1972, 1973, 1975, 1977, 1995 by The Lockman Foundation.

New International Reader's Version (NIRV) Copyright © 1996, 1998 by Biblica.

The Holy Bible, New International Version (NIV), Copyright © 1973, 1978, 1984, 2011 by Zondervan. All rights reserved.

The Holy Bible, New King James Version (NKJV) Copyright © 1982 by Thomas Nelson, Inc.

The Holy Bible, New Living Translation (NLT) Copyright © 1996, 2004, 2007 by Tyndale House Foundation. Used by permission of Tyndale House Publishers Inc., Carol Stream, Illinois 60188. All rights reserved.

Cover design: Gina Binkley
Book design: Glen Edelstein

Library of Congress Catalog-in-Publishing Data

Galasso-Vigorito, Catherine.
  The open window : 8 weeks to creating an extraordinary life / Catherine Galasso-Vigorito.
    p. cm.
ISBN 978-1-59652-896-3
1. Opportunity. 2. Success. I. Title.
B105.O67G35 2012
248.4--dc23
                              2012014463

Printed in the United States of America
12 13 14 15 16 17 18 0 9 8 7 6 5 4 3 2 1

To my husband, Todd,

and

our three beautiful daughters,

Lauren Grace, Gabriella, and Sophia:

May you always be on the lookout for the "open window" and

have the faith, courage, and fortitude to reach through.

I love you.

Ask, and it shall be given you;
seek; and you shall find;
knock and it shall be opened unto you."

MATTHEW 7:7

CONTENTS

Contents

ACKNOWLEGMENTS

"For where two or three are gathered together in my name, there am I in the midst of them." MATTHEW 18:20

With all my heart, I thank God for using me to encourage others with the encouragement that I was given.

I would like to extend my love and gratitude to Claire Gerus. Her belief, creative vision, and perseverance made *The Open Window* possible. She is a gift from God.

With appreciation to Ann Marie Brennan. She is always there for me, and her steadfast faith in God lights the way for all who come across her path.

My special thanks to publisher Todd Bottorff and his incredible, innovative team at Turner Publishing. Executive editor, the gracious Diane Gedymin: It has been a delight, an honor, and a pleasure working with you. Editor extraordinaire, Christina Huffines: I appreciate your kindness, invaluable advice, and enthusiasm for this project.

I'm also grateful to others at Turner Publishing who worked hard to produce *The Open Window*: outstanding cover designer Gina Binkley, artistic book designer Glen Edelstein, and fantastic copyeditor Ann Moller. You are all the best in the business.

My appreciation to William J. Rush, former publisher of the

New Haven Register, and to his wonderful wife, Ruth, who first gave me the opportunity to share my words and love for God with readers all over the country.

In fond remembrance of the late Robert M. Jelenic, former president and CEO of the Journal Register Company, for his support in the syndication of my newspaper column.

To Ray and Julie Cirmo, for their love and inspiration every day.

I am blessed to be surrounded by great friends and family: Kim McHenry, Kitty Law, Penelope Martin, Gia Calistro, Lucille Clancy, Thomas Draicchio, Vincent Farricelli, Jean Clifton, Jeff Chandler, Ginger Ballou, Aaron Bond, Bill Davidson, and Darlene Cavalier. They all inspire me with their hard work ethic, talents, and grace. They encouraged me tremendously during my book writing process.

Thank you to Scott Taylor, who always has the right words at the right time.

Thanks to Lexy Delvecchio, a beautiful young lady who helped me with my girls as I was composing *The Open Window.*

In loving memory of Major General William Cugno. I will never forget his kindness and for granting me the opportunity to write for a publication that encourages our brave servicemen and servicewomen.

With love and affection to my mother in heaven who gave me gifts that I will forever treasure and pass on to my children. And thank you to the precious readers of my newspaper columns and books, whose heartfelt letters have inspired me to write *The Open Window.*

INTRODUCTION

RECOGNIZE CLOSED DOORS
AS GOLDEN OPPORTUNITIES.

"And we know that in all things God works for the good of those who love Him, who have been called according to His purpose." ROMANS 8:28, NIV

I see the tears in people's eyes. And I feel the pain in their hearts. How do I know their anguish without their even saying a word? Because I, too, have been there.

But in each and every trial, whether tackling seemingly impossible situations or trying to stay afloat in a sea of difficulties, I can still hear my mother's melodic voice telling me: "When life closes a door, God always opens a window."

My mother's name was Elise, and she practiced this principle all of her life. And even though she has been gone from this earth for many years, I will forever remember her wise advice, and share that wisdom with others. For the open window never fails to appear *when we look for it,* inviting us to change our perspective and move with sure steps toward the divine destination God has chosen. All we need to do is to reach up and stretch our arms through that open window to embrace the new opportunities God is bringing our way.

In the Scriptures, God has promised that all things work

together for good to those who love Him and are called according to His purpose; moreover, that our challenges work *"for* us," not *"against* us." Although we may not see this or believe it at first, down the road we will know that these words are indeed true.

Therefore, when life closes a door:

✧ Will you trust God and persevere?

✧ Can you adjust your perspective and choose to see your challenges positively?

✧ Will you be patient and continue to praise God, allowing Him to do His work and bring you His rewards . . . in *His* time?

Consider that the choices you make, especially during challenging circumstances, will determine your life's course. Recognize that God may not always take you on the easy path. That is because He knows exactly what lessons you need to learn so you can develop to your full potential. That's why you cannot allow a disappointment, obstacle, or even a sequence of setbacks to convince you that your dreams are over. Actually, it's often a sign that they're on the verge of being realized.

In an eight-week program with a seven-day agenda, *The Open Window* is designed to provide you with a resource that can offer you immediate, workable suggestions, ideas, and concrete ways to help you to deal with the challenges of life.

You will discover within these pages stories of support and encouragement that reveal how times of adversity can really become windows of opportunity—if we're aware that a window has actually been opened. How do we know when the two events occur together? Because they always do!

Within this book, I'll reveal principles that can help you stay strong in difficult times. In addition, I will share personal moments from my own life, and stories from people just like you who persisted despite overwhelming situations. They were able to find their open windows, just as you will find those that are awaiting you.

So, step by step, let me help you to find your own "open window."

✧ Each morning, I'd like you to read one essay from the book. Reflect on what you've learned.

✧ Throughout the day, follow the advice and suggestions.

✧ Incorporate the action items into your life.

✧ The following morning, move on to the next essay.

"I learned this, at least, by my experiment; that if one advances confidently in the direction of his dreams and endeavors to live the life which he has imagined, he will meet with success unexpected in common hours."

HENRY DAVID THOREAU

Day by day, notice how you will begin to be filled with a newfound joy, as you discover that God is indeed with you, guiding you to a rich new life that will far exceed your expectations.

Share this journey with a friend or with a reading, support, or church group. Invite others to join in on the discussions. And I will be with you all the way.

Now, come along with me, follow the steps, read the stories within these pages, share the lessons herein with others, and know with certainty that you can achieve the life of your dreams—the new life you once only imagined.

May God bless you and keep you,
Catherine

THE OPEN WINDOW

WINDOW ONE

GET READY: CHANGE IS ON THE WAY!

"God, grant me the serenity to accept the things I cannot change,
the courage to change the things I can,
and the wisdom to know the difference."

FROM *THE SERENITY PRAYER*

DAY ONE:

TODAY IS THE DAY TO BEGIN TO DISCOVER YOUR PURPOSE.

"Trust in the Lord with all your heart, and lean not on your own understanding; in all your ways acknowledge Him, and He shall direct your paths." PROVERBS 3:5-6, NKJV

"Mommy, when will it be summer?" asked Sophia, my almost-four-year-old daughter. She was sitting on the couch, bundled in a green woolen blanket, and her bright blue eyes regarded me with eager anticipation.

"Summer will be here in just a few months, Sophia," I replied matter-of-factly, knowing what was on her mind. The temperature was 32 degrees outside and Sophia was yearning for warmer weather. She longed to go to the playground, swim at the seashore, and visit her favorite carousel. "But that will be for-e-e-ever," she responded, with a big grin, her eyebrows scrunching into her little nose.

I had to smile, for I knew exactly how she felt. Sophia's question suddenly brought back cherished memories: our family gathering seashells together on the beach, with the August sand under our feet. Then, in mid-October, we'd see gold and crimson leaves adorning the trees, as we drove to an orchard to pick baskets of juicy apples. Squirrels gathered their precious acorn treasures, and we would shiver when the night air brought its crispy chill, heralding autumn's arrival.

After that, as swiftly as a turn of a page in a book, came winter. And with it, the unsurpassed beauty of the season's first gentle flakes of snow. Chimneys blazed in the evening and my husband, Todd, our three daughters, and I would nestle together by a cozy fire. Watching the flames in the fireplace, we'd reflect on how thankful we were for the gift of love in our lives.

As I write these words in the heart of New England, it's almost springtime, and the promise of change is all around us. I once heard someone say, "If nothing ever changed, there would be no butterflies." Oh, how true. And like the butterfly that emerges triumphantly from its chrysalis, you, too, can experience the satisfaction of transforming into a newer, brighter individual in God's great universe.

"Observe always that everything is the result of change, and get used to thinking that there is nothing Nature loves so well as to change existing forms and make new ones like them."

MARCUS AURELIUS

Now, it's time for you to awaken yourself to new directions and new possibilities. It is time to uncover your hidden gifts and move forward, opening up your arms to receive the utmost in love, health, peace, happiness, and success.

It's the season to lie in the grass, study the clouds, plan, and dream. It's a time of contemplation, of reflection: on where you've been and what you have learned, and where you are going next.

What are the truths of your heart? I'm asking you to take a good, long look at your life and carve out the time to invest in discovering your divine purpose. The important thing is to be totally honest with yourself, as you utilize this transformative season as an opportunity to ask yourself three questions:

1. What would I pursue if anything were possible?
2. Am I utilizing to the fullest the gifts that God has given to me?
3. Who do I want to be?

There is no set path or answers—just listen to the dreams of your heart. Today is the day to begin to live the life that you want to live and truly pursue what you would like to do.

Next, I'd like you to get a pencil and a sheet of paper, sit down in a comfortable chair, and start by writing a one-sentence definition for your

"Twenty years from now you will be more disappointed by the things that you didn't do than by the ones you did do. So throw off the bowlines. Sail away from the safe harbor. Catch the trade winds in your sails. Explore. Dream. Discover."

MARK TWAIN

life—a mission statement. Really evaluate your priorities and write a list of five to ten aspirations for the future. Set your goals in motion by writing them out in complete detail. Let's say you aspire to own your own home. Write out details about this home: the style, color, location. Or if you want to get married, list attributes that you are looking for in a soul mate.

Challenge the status quo, get out of your comfort zone, and let your imagination go. Dare to dream, reaching as high as your imagination will take you.

Beside the objectives, jot down dates by which your desired aspirations should be accomplished. Then, start believing in your

God-given abilities and acting upon them to see them come to life, for action will get you to your goals. In your mind, visualize the completed aspirations. And affirm daily their realization, while keeping your self-talk positive.

Place your "Aspiration List" where you can view it each morning and evening. And as situations reveal themselves, adjust or modify your list accordingly. You could also schedule time to modify or adjust it bimonthly, regardless of external circumstances.

"To change one's life: 1. Start immediately.
2. Do it flamboyantly. 3. No exceptions."

WILLIAM JAMES

You were not born to sit in the audience and see your life pass by, as if you were watching a theater performance. You have a great and important role to play. Therefore, emerge from behind the curtain, take center stage, and share your extraordinary gifts with the world.

God had a great purpose in mind when He created you, and He gave you everything you need to contribute to a cause greater than yourself. The Bible says:

"Each one should use whatever gift he has received to serve others,
faithfully administering God's grace in its various forms"

(1 PETER 4:10, NIV).

"And God is able to make all grace abound to you, so that in all things
at all times, having all that you need, you will abound in
every good work"

(2 CORINTHIANS 9:8, NIV).

8

The Open Window

"Because of God's tender mercy, the morning light from heaven is about to break upon us"

(LUKE 1:78, NLT).

Each sunrise is a chance to start over with new potential and promise. So begin today by saying: *This is my day of opportunity.* Then, go out and begin to pursue your passions.

✧ Dream a new dream and do one thing today to start to make it come true.

✧ Set a creative thought into motion. If you aspire to take that new class, sign up now.

✧ Send a note or call someone who may be able to positively influence your future.

✧ Maybe there is something you want to change about yourself. First, start on the inside by "acting like" the person you desire to be. Have faith in God, pray for help in discovering your purpose, and believe . . . and the rest will follow.

In the Scriptures, when Jesus healed the blind man, He needed the man's cooperation for the man to be changed. Jesus asked, "What wilt thou that I should do unto thee?" The blind man said unto Him, "Lord, that I might receive my sight" (Mark 10:46-52). It was the blind man's faith in Jesus that allowed him to be healed. Therefore, when we request something of God, we too, must have faith and believe. God can transform us in this life; if we are first willing do our part.

Think about sweet, soft baby eaglets. The mother eagle cares for and nurtures her beloved offspring. Yet, when the time comes for the eaglets to grow up and fly on their own, they are pushed out of their nest. As they try to hold on to their mother, not wanting to alter their comfortable environment, she gently shakes her

Keep in mind that most brilliant changes require a time of discomfort. Yet, for the most part, discomfort is usually a good sign, for it means that you are getting somewhere.

babies loose, forcing them to fly. The eaglets stretch their wings in response to the direction of the wind and soar into adulthood as the mighty eagles God intended them to be.

Are you, like the eaglets, experiencing a situation that is uncomfortable? Perhaps the change you are confronted with right now can be the impetus for your greatest achievements. Regardless of past circumstances, God has placed the power within you to create a better life. And just as the majestic eagle was created to soar far above the plains below, higher and higher into the azure sky, you have much further to go on your journey.

Go ahead: Dream, discover, prepare, plan, and believe. A whole new clear, glorious life lies before you.

DAY TWO:

ACCEPT THE UNKNOWNS WITH CONFIDENCE.

"The Sovereign Lord is my strength; He makes my feet like the feet of a deer, He enables me to go on the heights."
HABAKKUK 3:19, NIV

The Book of Ruth is a story about change. It opens with the sad death of Ruth's husband, but it later unfolds to reveal the triumph of God's grace in the midst of changing circumstances beyond Ruth's control.

Ruth, a Moabite widow, had selflessly refused to leave her mother-in-law, Naomi, alone after Naomi's husband's death, proclaiming the timeless words:

"Do not urge me to leave you or to return from following you. For where you go I will go, and where you lodge I will lodge. Your people shall be my people, and your God my God"

(RUTH 1:16-17, ESV).

When Ruth left her family and the familiarity of her homeland to accompany Naomi to Bethlehem, she had accepted the unknowns that lay before them. The two women arrived in Bethlehem poor and hungry. But they did not just sit back and expect events to simply happen. To obtain food, young Ruth gleaned the ground for morsels of grain in vast fields owned by a wealthy man named Boaz.

And, to their amazement, Boaz turned out to be a relative of Naomi's, and when he heard of Ruth's kindness to her mother-in-law, Boaz instructed his workers to leave grain behind for her to gather. Boaz himself was very kind to Ruth and encouraged her to collect food from his fields. Before long, Boaz obtained the blessing of the elders to take Ruth to be his wife.

Their union was a joyous one, and later she gave birth to a healthy son. Change had led to glory, and Ruth's tears of sorrow became tears of gratitude.

Now, think about the unknowns you have encountered in your own life. How did they turn out? For example, when you finished school and didn't find a job right away, what happened? What about when you moved to a new city? Looking back, how did the transition work out? When you got married, that was an

In a journal, keep a record of the unknowns that you have faced in the past. What happened in each of these circumstances? Now, write down the unknowns that you are facing currently. Next, compile a list of problems resulting from a current circumstance, like an illness, a rejection, or a loss. Did something good come out of those events? How has change become a *positive force* in your life?

unknown. What about when you had children? All of our major life events involve unknowns, right?

Some time ago, I received a letter from a reader I'll call Janet. Janet wrote that three years ago she was diagnosed with lung cancer. Thankfully, it was caught early. But just when she thought one problem was solved, the following fall she was diagnosed with breast cancer. Once again, by God's grace, it was caught very early. Still, she had to undergo surgery, chemotherapy, and radiation. Unfortunately, while she was trying to regain her health, her marriage crumbled. The pain was great. Although she prayed earnestly, she ended up going through a divorce. However, Janet did not become embittered with all the unknowns and changes; she responded to all these struggles with trust, and as a result, her faith in God grew. Janet looked to and depended on God, knowing that He is in complete control and that He loves each of us. Indeed, God brought good out of a difficult situation, as her past suffering has turned to new joy.

Janet shared that now she is the happiest she has ever been in her life, living in a peaceful home, with a rewarding career and many faithful friends. Her letter concluded, "I wanted to send you a big thank you, Catherine, for helping me through these last three difficult years. I cannot express enough to you the strength your weekly messages provided me. I'm sure you've helped so many others like myself."

If you are overwhelmed with indecision and unknowns about your future, ask God for guidance by trying this approach:

1. Turn off the television, radio, your computer, and your cell phone—any distractions.
2. After that, sit comfortably in a quiet, peaceful spot at the park, the beach, or in your yard. Being close to nature is therapeutic.
3. Clear your mind of everything else, breathe in, and exhale slowly, for inner peace comes when your mind settles and stays quiet.

4. Now, close your eyes and focus your attention on God.
5. Once you feel completely relaxed and stress-free, ask God for what you desire, whether it is guidance for a particular issue or help with an unknown or a problem.
6. Then, imagine yourself as you would like to be, and the matter successfully resolved.

Practice this method daily or weekly to lessen anxiety and strengthen your relationship with God. Have faith; God will send the answer to you, for He will never let you down.

> *"Frequently remind yourself that God is with you, that He will never fail you, that you can count upon Him. Say these words, 'God is with me, helping me.'"*

NORMAN VINCENT PEALE

Last week, I was talking to a long-time friend who now lives in Europe. She recalled, "My darkest days were when I was getting my divorce." And then she told me how her ex-husband had taken what little remained in a small bank account for their daughter, and left her with thousands of dollars of debt—a house in the city that needed much work, a car that didn't work, a six-year-old child who needed care after school and in the summer—and she was only earning $16,000 a year.

With unshakeable trust in God, my friend declared, "If anyone had told me then that my daughter would go on to be a lawyer, living in a beautiful home, and that I would be living in Europe and be an executive of a major corporation—I would have never believed it. But it happened. God took care of things."

Memorize this quote and repeat it when you're up against an unknown circumstance: "When life closes a door, God always opens a window." Then, be on the lookout. You can see it when a person loses a job and finds a better one. Or a relationship ends, only to discover a new love. The old door closed, and a window opened up to a new opportunity . . . most times better than the last.

Honor unknowns by casting all your cares upon God, because He cares so much for you. And today, read over this Scripture in the morning, at noon, and again before bedtime: "So do not fear, for I am with you; do not be dismayed, for I am your God. I will strengthen you and help you; I will uphold you with my righteous right hand. All who rage against you will surely be ashamed and disgraced; those who oppose you will be as nothing and perish. Though you search for your enemies, you will not find them. Those who wage war against you will be as nothing at all. For I am the Lord, your God, who takes hold of your right hand and says to you, 'Do not fear; I will help you'" (Isaiah 41:10-13, NIV).

DAY THREE:

YESTERDAY'S PAIN WILL OPEN A WINDOW TO A FUTURE FILLED WITH HOPE.

"The steadfast love of the Lord never ceases, his mercies never come to an end; they are new every morning."
LAMENTATIONS 3:22-23, ESV

In 1929, the economic downturn of the Great Depression caused a major financial disaster for businessman James Cash Penney. Due to his bad investments in real estate and banking, the strain of the financial collapse took its toll on the 56-year-old entrepreneur's health. Weakened in mind, body, and spirit, Penney was filled with despair and was soon hospitalized.

It seemed as though his plans, his dreams, and his life were finished. Yet, you can't keep a good, honorable person down, for God can send people in our direction to help us overcome difficulties. Or He can send inspirational thoughts or words our way that speak to our hearts, allowing us to connect to the strength we need to rise up again.

One day, while Penney was being treated in the hospital, he heard some music coming from the hospital's small chapel. The encouraging words of the melody caught his attention: *"Be not dismayed, what-e'er betide. God will take care of you . . ."*

Hearing these words was a turning point in Penney's life. He felt the hope of God. And almost instantaneously, the businessman was lifted from hopelessness to hopefulness, from inner turmoil to quiet trust.

Thereafter, Penney decided to start over. He went back to work. And before long, he was able to regain control of his empire, and the J. C. Penney's chain of department stores became one of the most successful retail establishments in America. Moreover, Penney gave millions to charities around the globe.

Later, when J. C. Penney reflected on his life, he said, "I believe in adherence to the Golden Rule, faith in God and the country. If I were a young man again, those would be my cardinal principles." God had a new start for J. C. Penney and, likewise, He has another dream and more victories to come for you.

"Let go of the past and go for the future. Go confidently in the direction of your dreams. Live the life you imagined."

HENRY DAVID THOREAU

Are you looking for a new beginning in your life? Do you want to wipe the slate clean and make a fresh start in your career, relationships, or health? Will you be turning off of the highway you've been traveling on, and taking another path? Think of starting over as an exciting new adventure by:

- ✧ First: Making a commitment.
- ✧ Second: Learning from the past, accepting what transpired, and moving forward.
- ✧ Third: Mapping out a plan of action in writing and following it.

17

❖ Fourth: Expecting that your new venture will, in its own timetable, reveal great rewards.

❖ Fifth: Pushing through the door called "fear" by trusting in God and His perfect timing.

"You will go out in joy and be led forth in peace; the mountains and hills will burst into song before you, and all the trees of the field will clap their hands."

IsaIah 55:12, NIV

The Lord said to Abraham: "Lift up your eyes from where you are and look north and south, east and west. All the land that you see I will give to you and your offspring forever" (Genesis 13:14, NIV). You, too, must lift your eyes from where you are now, and look out to where you want to be. Remember, God is in charge and is working situations out on His own calendar and in His own mighty way, as He did in the life of Rebekah in the Old Testament.

In those times, the main purpose of a woman's life was to get married and bear children, for children were the hope of the future. However, Rebekah was unable to have a child. But her husband, Isaac, prayed, asking for a son (Genesis 25:21). God heard Isaac's prayer, and soon, Rebekah gave birth to twin boys, who they named Jacob and Esau. As He did for Rebekah and Isaac, God can go above and beyond to give you what's best for your future.

Recently, neighbors of ours traveled to Paris—a trip for which they had been planning for years. When they returned, my family and I went to their home to watch a slide show of their fabulous trip. As we sat there on the leather couch and viewed the photographs, there were sights from Italy, Spain, and Germany.

"I thought you only went to France?" I asked, a bit confused.

"Well, that was our original plan," the wife revealed. "However, our tour guide suggested that we make some changes to our itinerary to enhance our trip, and to make it more memorable."

With a flash of certainty, she declared, "We decided to take the tour guide's advice. He knows best, after all, so we followed his lead."

Just as the tour guide changed our neighbor's travel plans, as we progress on our life's journey, God alters certain circumstances for our greater good. Thus, let us trust Him, for God sees the whole picture. *He knows best*, so let's follow *His lead*. And similar to the tour guide, God does not take us on alternate routes or hinder our plans to ruin the trip, but to enhance our journey and make it more memorable.

> *"When you cannot make up your mind which*
> *of two evenly balanced courses of action*
> *you should take—choose the bolder."*
>
> WILLIAM JOSEPH SLIM

Whether it's your first attempt to achieve something extraordinary or only a change of plans, a delay, or a redirection in your life, do not permit fear to fill your heart. I believe some opportunities are coming your way. Be open to those possibilities. For soon, God will bless your efforts, a window will open, and you will be accelerated ahead. Have confidence. With God, there is no limit as to what you can accomplish, except the limits that you place on yourself.

Trust that everything will turn out right. You're a star in God's great universe and you are meant to shine!

DAY FOUR:

LET GOD'S PLAN TRANSFORM YOUR LIFE.

"For I know the plans I have for you, declares the Lord, plans to
prosper you and not to harm you, plans to give you hope and a future."
JEREMIAH 29:11, NIV

One afternoon, I received a powerful letter from a husband and wife who wrote to tell me that each week they cut out my column and mail it to their teenage daughter, who is in reform school. "My daughter says that your articles help her to see the true light God shines on all of us," the father shared.

Next, the father went on to explain in the four-page letter that their daughter had been very destructive and out of control. Her situation appeared to be almost impossible to surmount. But the parents had stood strong, and found a school a few states over to help their child with her mounting challenges. Now, their daughter is getting much-needed support and assistance through this school's fine program.

The father wrote that, as his daughter reaches for recovery, she knows that God is with her, right by her side, as God's love reaches into the future and knows no boundaries. That knowledge alone

For major life changes or crises, seek a professional. Workplace counselors, community groups, family services departments, churches, and schools often provide therapy, counselors, and support groups to help people.

causes this young woman to have hope and a brighter outlook for the days to come.

And one day at a time, she is developing into a loving, caring, appreciative person. Indeed, she is picking up the pieces of her life and putting them back together, and in the process, she is an inspiration to those around her. As difficult as her circumstances have been, this teen is emerging triumphantly. Her parents suggest to her often, "The past is behind you and it can't be changed. So live for today, learn from yesterday, and have hope for tomorrow." This story inspired me and I pray that by God's grace this young lady continues to change and shape her life in a positive direction.

One way to cope with change is to develop a network of encouraging friends and caring relatives who will provide companionship, listen, and simply be there when you need support.

Are their areas in your life where you need help? Do you think you have exhausted all of your resources? Well, you haven't. You are a survivor. There is no problem that you cannot conquer, no negative history you cannot overcome, and no dream that you cannot achieve. Life is about choices. And each decision you make creates *you*.

Therefore, you can choose to start over, to change directions, and to strive to attain your heart's highest goal. Try this: Ask God to help you, then forge ahead, " . . . reaching forth unto those things which are before [you]," and you will triumph (Philippians 3:13).

The Bible describes the transformation of a man named Zacchaeus, a very wealthy senior tax collector and therefore not well-liked in the town. Beginning in Luke 19, Scriptures tell how Jesus was passing through Jericho and Zacchaeus was eager to catch a glimpse of him. There were many people gathered around to see Jesus, and because Zacchaeus was a short man, he decided to climb a tree to be able to get a better look. "When Jesus came to the tree, he looked up and said, 'Zacchaeus, hurry and come down, for I must stay at your house today'" (19:5, ESV).

Zacchaeus then came down from the tree, "received him joyfully," and instantly became a changed man. In fact, he gave half his money to the poor and said that if he had cheated anyone in the past, he would pay them back four times the amount he'd cheated them out of. Zacchaeus had been transformed, just by seeing Jesus from high up in a sycamore tree.

So, do not stay where you are, sitting idly because you are paralyzed by mistakes of long ago. You can change, too. A part of getting over the past is relishing in the "here and now." It's time to get up and get moving, and take a leap of faith. And watch, in awe, at what God will do as His plans for you unfold.

Look toward your goals, see yourself going further, aim higher, and your life will follow that vision. The direction of your focus is the direction in which your life will go.

Last week, I was at the store selecting a greeting card for my daughter Gabriella's upcoming birthday. I lingered for a time, opening up card after card, and soon a cashier walked over to me and asked, "Do you need any help?" Smiling, I explained, "I'm looking for the perfect birthday card for my little girl, to let her know that, year after year, I love her more and more." That's how God feels about you, for you are His beloved child, and with each passing moment, He loves you more and more.

What if I asked you to think about what you could accomplish if you saw yourself through God's eyes? Why don't you try it now? Silence the internal voices in your head, trying to pigeonhole you, which may utter, "You're not good enough," "You can't do that," or "You've made too many mistakes." And in their place, trust in God totally, and many times throughout the day reflect on God's word, which says:

✦ "In Him we have redemption through His blood, the forgiveness of sins, in accordance with the riches of God's grace." EPHESIANS 1:7, NIV

✦ "Your eyes saw my substance, being yet unformed. And in Your book they were all written, the days fashioned for me, when as yet there were none of them." PSALM 139:16, NKJV

✦ "Delight thyself also in the Lord: and He shall give thee the desires of thine heart." PSALM 37:4

✦ "For we know, brothers and sisters loved by God, that He has chosen you." 1 THESSALONIANS 1:4, ESV

Choose to use each and every day well, and to fill your precious hours with love, purpose, joy, and peace. God is smiling down on you today. Let Him transform your life.

DAY FIVE:

BELIEVE IN YOURSELF AND START LOVING YOU.

"You are my handiwork, created to produce good works which I prepared in advance for you to do."
EPHESIANS 2:10, NIV

Growing in lakes and marshes, with its roots digging deep into the soil, the lotus flower slowly rises. Although the lotus has its beginnings at the bottom, in the mud's murky darkness, because of its natural strength, the flower ascends above the water's surface. With its pink petals leaning toward the sun, the lotus sits elegantly, blooming with unsurpassed grace and beauty.

Have you been dealt a pointless and unproductive blow? Has someone crippled your momentum? Is the greatness that you have within you hiding behind your fears? Could you be blocking your own blessings because you do not feel worthy?

When I see a lotus bloom on the glistening waters of our lake, I am reminded to continue to strive through difficulties. And like the lotus flower, with God's grace, you will emerge triumphantly from the murky darkness into the bright light of the sun.

Be confident in who you are and where you are going! From

God's perspective, as He reveals to us in Ephesians 2:10, "You are my handiwork, created to produce good works which I prepared in advance for you to do." You are fully adequate, competent, and worthy. So, you need to see the worth in yourself that God sees in you. Trust and have confidence in your own brilliance. Be true to yourself. And recognize your great God-inspired potential.

Embrace yourself and ask, "What makes me, *me*?" Then, write in a diary five qualities you like about yourself. Tomorrow, jot down another quality and so forth. Reread your list at the end of the week for a source of encouragement. You're one-of-a-kind, an irreplaceable and special person. So move beyond self-imposed boundaries that have tried to hedge you in. Then, carry your calling forward, not wasting another moment in self-defeating habits, self-pity, or self-deprivation.

I once read a narrative about an artist who had a burst of inspiration, and was in urgent need of some paper on which to sketch it. There was no drawing paper or sketchbook within easy reach, so he took an ordinary sheet of wrapping paper, turned it over, and, with pencil in hand, he drew a picture. With quiet joy, he created exquisite lines until they took form, and skillfully outlined gracious curves on the wrapping paper, opening his heart to the inspiration of the moment.

The sketch wonderfully emerged into a fine composition, and

thereafter his creation was displayed in an art exhibit with a brief story attached, explaining how his design had come to fruition. Standing by the drawing and gazing at it closely, a woman asked the artist how he created such a beautiful work of art on an ordinary sheet of wrapping paper.

The artist replied, "It does not matter what the outside *appears* to be. I looked beyond the outer surface, for I knew a masterpiece was hidden within." That is how God views you: He sees the masterpiece within. You were born to make a difference, to give this world something that no one else can.

How do you love "you"? Actress Lucille Ball said, "Love yourself first and everything falls into line." Loving "who you are" begins by making a conscious decision to allow yourself to lead a full, joyous, and productive life.

1. Nurture yourself on all levels: physically, mentally, and spiritually. Carry out at least one enjoyable activity each day that is exclusively for your own self-nurturing.

2. Eliminate self-criticism and negative self-dialogue, and in their place, express gratitude for the person that you are and for the person that you're becoming.

3. Stop comparing yourself to others. Remind yourself that there's only one "you" and thus, you have a unique combination of gifts that others do not possess.

Young Mary was in her early teens when an angel appeared to her and said, ". . . thou that art highly favored, the Lord is with thee: blessed art thou among women" (Luke 1:28). The angel told Mary not to fear, and that she would have a baby who would be God's son. "And, behold, thou shalt conceive in thy womb, and bring forth a son, and shalt call his name Jesus" (Luke 1:31).

Rather than thinking she was not good or worthy enough for such a momentous assignment, Mary replied in a statement of faith, "Behold the handmaid of the Lord; be it unto me according to thy word" (Luke 1:38). In other words, Mary lived her life in obedience to God and was willing to do what He asked of her. Just as with Mary, God looks at our obedience and faith, often selecting and using the unlikeliest of choices, to fulfill His magnificent plans.

I recently read about a young woman named Jen, who was born with SED, a genetic mutation that leads to abnormal collagen formation. This rare bone growth disorder caused dwarfism in Jen, as well as other complications that have required her to endure more than 30 complicated surgeries.

We can all find excuses not to love ourselves. Some people are stopped by fear. Others are halted by thoughts of deprivation. Or they refuse to accept the changes that they have to endure. Yet Jen never lets her challenges or small stature allow her to stop loving and believing in herself, or to let her precious life pass her by.

Instead, she believes that her dreams are all attainable. Jen's motto is: "Think big to overcome obstacles!" She has met the challenges of change with a positive attitude, choosing to be filled with joy, spunk, and enthusiasm. With a beautiful smile on her face the vast majority of days, Jen is kind to others, self-assured, and determined to live productively.

*"Take full account of what excellencies which
you possess, and in gratitude remember how you
would hanker after them, if you had them not."*

MARCUS AURELIUS

If Jen comes across a difficulty, such as what to wear, how to drive a car, or what to do when she goes out to eat in a restaurant, she doesn't dwell on the stumbling blocks. She modifies her surroundings—shopping in children's clothing stores, using a pedal extender to drive, and propping herself up on pillows in restaurants to enjoy her meal.

Over the years, Jen decided to fulfill her aspiration to go to college. She refused to listen to the word "no," and instead set her sights on giving back to the world. Then, after graduation, Jen attended medical school, specializing in caring for the smallest babies in the neonatal unit. An inspiration to all, Jen sees no barriers!

Today, standing at three feet, two inches tall, in her custom-made white coat, Dr. Jennifer Arnold is a highly trained pediatrician, a neonatal specialist, and an assistant professor of pediatrics. In addition, she recently got married. She and her new husband, Bill, built a new home and they're planning to start a family.

Moreover, this couple has their own hit television show on TLC. And I believe that this is only the beginning of the blessings that God has in store for this remarkable woman!

*"May the Lord bless you from Zion
all the days of your life."*

PSALM 128:5, NIV

Recognize your self-worth, for God has put you here on earth to be happy and to succeed in all that you undertake. And like the exquisite lotus flower, you will come out from the murky waters, rising up stronger, wiser, and better equipped for your amazing victory ahead.

Day six:

Make time for what matters most.

"I will instruct you and teach you in the way you shall go;
I will guide you with my eye."
PSALM 32:8, NKJV

After a long, cold winter, it was wonderful to be outdoors in front of our home. The sun warmed my face and I bent down and picked up a handful of rich soil and let it run through my fingers to the ground. I heard the birds' melodic song and felt the gentle breeze on my back, as I began to plant bouquets of hardy purple and white pansies in our garden. And I recalled an ancient Chinese saying that I like:

Ten thousand flowers in the spring,
the moon in autumn,
a cool breeze in summer,
snow in winter.
If your mind isn't clouded by unnecessary things,
this is the best season of your life.
—Sage Wu Men

A few minutes later, my giggling children, with their colorful kite strings in hand, ran across the green grass and a patch of buttercups in the front yard, in an effort to gain enough momentum for their kites to soar to great heights and fly.

Days stretch into months, and months into years, and sometimes, because of the many difficulties that come upon us, it is easy to get discouraged and forget that each moment we live is a treasure, a gift. But we must cherish these special days. And although we may not be able to change what has happened in the past, like my children flying their kites, we have the power to soar far above our challenges, and make this very minute, this day, and this new, glorious season, the *best* of our lives.

Has an unexpected life change thrown you off balance? Whether it's the end of a relationship, job, or lifestyle, in the winds of change, you can discover your real friends, steadfast faith, unwavering strength, newfound happiness, increased wisdom, and your true destiny.

Shed those tears and smile again. God is a God of another chance. There is so much more yet to come for you. Today, I'm asking you to thank God for all He has given to you, and to praise Him for all the good that He plans on bringing into your future.

I like the story about a wealthy city executive who took his wife and daughter on a weekend trip to the country. The executive had all the material possessions you can imagine, but he worked all the time and hardly ever spent any time with his loved ones. So one weekend, instead of staying at an extravagant hotel, he decided to take his family to spend Saturday and Sunday on a farm with a very poor family to teach his daughter what it was like to be poor.

When they returned to their lavish home, this executive asked his daughter, "How did you like our little trip to the country?"

The daughter responded, "Oh, I loved it, Dad!"

Then, he inquired, "What did you learn?" and "Did you find out just how poor people live?"

Grinning from ear to ear, the daughter replied, "The family we stayed with was kind and giving. I saw how they worked together; they took care of their many animals and ate fresh food that they grew in their garden. For fun, they took walks in the fresh air of the countryside, tossed a ball around with their dog, and swam at a lake near their home. And at night, I liked how they ate dinner together, played games, sang songs, talked, and laughed with each other."

The executive didn't say a word.

And then his daughter uttered sincerely, "Thank you, Dad, for showing me just how poor *we* are."

Begin today by asking yourself, "During these changing times, am I looking around to see what is truly important?" "Where am I spending my time and energy?" "Am I creating time for what matters most: my faith, relationships, my health, hobbies, and passions?" and "What do I want to do that I never have time for?"

"Time flies, but remember, you are the navigator."

AUTHOR UNKNOWN

Each Sunday, sit down with a daily planner and practice these seven simple steps to add meaningful moments to your days:

1. Think about how you currently spend your week.
2. Identify activities that are optional, such as watching television.

3. Set limits. You don't have to attend every party or function. Organize your priorities, so you can truly enjoy the events you choose to attend and the activities you choose to partake in.

4. Next, jot down things that you love to do. Maybe you and your family enjoy attending sporting events or concerts. Do you like cooking with an innovative recipe? Or participating in a hobby or a personal training session? Perhaps you want to pursue a long-held dream, revive a forgotten one, or attempt to try something new?

5. Once you've uncovered what you are passionate about, ask, "How can I bring more of these things into my daily life?" "What can I schedule in now, this week or this month?"

6. Now, in a daily planner, identify your work responsibilities and all that you absolutely must do.

7. Next, arrange your schedule to allot time to the people, activities, and events that matter most to you.

Despite who you are and no matter what you have been through, in your hands is the power to make change happen and create time for what matters most. How? Stop thinking about yesterday's regrets and mistakes. In its place, focus on the positive aspects of your life right now and the wonderful things you are looking forward to welcoming into your future.

Has a window closed? Refocus your efforts on something new:

✧   Go on a spiritual retreat to gain insight and develop solutions to issues.

✧   Change your thinking pattern by drawing your thoughts away from the past and back to the present.

✧   Accept that what took place before cannot be changed. Rather than mulling over previous disappointments, consider the lessons learned, opportunities provided, and achievements yet to come.

✧ Get involved in other projects. Keep busy pursuing worthwhile aspirations.

✧ Initiate new friendships and connections with people by volunteering.

Bring happiness to others wherever it is possible. Give a compliment. Do a good deed every day. Smile more often. Express to your loved ones how much you care. Be resolute in fostering harmonious home surroundings. Lift up a friend in need. Slow down and spend time in nature. Participate in a regular fitness routine and eat nutritious, quality food. And if you can, adopt a pet and experience unconditional love and laughter. This is a new day—and there is no better time than right now to reach for your best life.

So, let's make the most of each moment and adhere to what the Scriptures say:

"Teach us to number our days, that we may apply our hearts unto wisdom" (Psalm 90:12).

"Therefore be careful how you walk, not as unwise men, but as wise men making the most of your time" (Ephesians 5:15, NASB).

"Do unto others as you would have them do to you" (Luke 6:31, NIV).

"Be wise in the way you act toward outsiders; make the most of every opportunity. Let your conversation be always full of grace, seasoned with salt, so that you may know how to answer everyone" (Colossians 4:5-6, NIV).

"This is the day that the Lord has made; let us rejoice and be glad in it" (Psalm 118:24, ESV).

"I am only one, but still I am one. I cannot do everything, but still I can do something; and because I cannot do everything, I will not refuse to do something that I can do."

EDWARD EVERETT HALE

As you explore more of the Bible, you will find that God wants you to experience the tremendous joys of life.

I'm hoping that you will follow your passions and have the courage to pursue goals that you may have previously thought of as mere dreams. Be bold and challenge yourself to try new things. Trying something different gets you out of your rut and can fill your life with interesting experiences. Small changes can make a big difference. Therefore, start now! Develop the unwavering belief, "I can do anything that I put my mind to do." Then, go forth, and with each magnificent sunrise, you'll begin to accomplish your heart's desires, and become more joyful and balanced. This is your year, this is your day . . . this is the *best season* of your life . . . embrace it!

DAY SEVEN:

IN THE FACE OF CHANGE, TAKE CARE OF YOUR PHYSICAL HEALTH.

"I beseech you therefore, brethren, by the mercies of God, that ye present your bodies a living sacrifice, holy, acceptable unto God, which is your reasonable service."

ROMANS 12:1

Framed in my office is a greeting card that reads, "The difficulties we face can be used as stepping-stones, guiding us to the place God wants us to be."

Six years ago, I experienced a difficult change. I had medical complications after giving birth to our third daughter, and while recuperating, I was torn between whether I should resume my long-standing career in radio or stay at home with the children. "While home with the girls," I pondered, "I could more actively engage in my writing and even develop inspirational products and a show that could help others."

But the idea of a career change was terrifying, and those thoughts were tearfully followed by questions like: *"Why would you leave the security of a steady paycheck?" "How can you give up all of those accounts you worked for 12 years to build?" "What about the children's future?"*

Although progress is impossible without change, we must first ask God how we can best accomplish that change according to His will. So one day in prayer, I asked, *"Lord, what do you want me to do?"* Listening intently, I heard His guidance: *"I will make a way . . . remember, you work for Me."*

Shortly afterward, releasing what seemed to be safety in order to embrace the new, I resigned from my corporate job. And I realized what a treasure I now had before me: the ability to stay home with my daughters while continuing to pursue my writing career and carry on sharing my messages of hope.

For me, a longtime career girl, changing directions was tremendously difficult, and without my corporate profession, my sense of self-worth dropped drastically. However, one of the best things that helped me in my transition from corporate lifestyle to stay-at-home mom was exercise! At Christmas, my husband, Todd, gave me a membership to the local fitness center. In the past, I had always exercised, yet over the last few years, I'd been so busy with family and career that I'd stopped following a regular routine.

And so, one cold winter morning, I bundled up little Sophia and we went to the local exercise class. There was a day-care center at the gym run by local moms, so Sophia stayed with them for the hour, playing with the other children.

> *"A vigorous five-mile walk will do more good for an unhappy but otherwise healthy adult than all the medicine and psychology in the world."*
>
> PAUL DUDLEY WHITE, AMERICAN PHYSICIAN AND CARDIOLOGIST

Attending that exercise class turned out to be a dramatic support for my career changes, and it helped me weather the daily ups and downs of my new lifestyle. Master teacher Michelle Cretella was my instructor, and one of the most enthusiastic and motivational people I have ever met. As she taught the class and we followed her every step, she spoke words of hope to us:

"You are not defined by where you are now, but by the path you are taking," she shouted above the loud music as we trained. "Success is getting up one more time when you have fallen down," she'd tell us when we faltered with an exercise.

"'Good enough' just isn't," Michelle would insist, urging us to go further than we thought possible. "There is no tomorrow, so you must work hard today," she would call out. "You set the pace for your life, so wake up every day and believe that anything is possible!" "Now is not the time to quit," she would encourage as we labored on the exercise floor.

At that time, everything seemed overwhelming, but I also knew that God was in control of my endeavors. It had been He who had put the dreams I most cherished within my heart, and I believed that ultimately He would make the wrongs right.

When I looked around me in the exercise room, I saw others who were struggling with change, too: a young woman who had lost a beloved parent, another with problems in her marriage, a man with ongoing health problems, and a woman who confided in me that her husband had been out of work for years. However, with each jumping jack, hop, step, and stomp, I could tell their strength was increased and their optimism renewed—just as mine was. Everything seemed different.

That class was one of the things that helped me make better nutritional choices, keep "spiritually fit" as well as physically fit, and prepare me for future transformations.

When was the last time that you spent an hour a day on your physical well-being? With a physician's okay, I'd like you to engage in activities regularly that you enjoy. Schedule your workout in your planner, as you would an appointment, and abide by it.

✧ Find a friend and try jogging or speed walking.

✧ Buy yourself a new exercise outfit and the right footwear, and participate in an aerobics, Pilates, or step aerobics group workout.

- ✧ If you like to dance, take Zumba classes.
- ✧ Play golf or a game of tennis with your spouse.
- ✧ Wake up an hour earlier and walk on a treadmill, so you can exercise regardless of the weather.
- ✧ Take a bike ride or go on a hike with your family on the weekends.

If something is weighing on your mind, go on a long walk by yourself so you will have time to think and begin to work through whatever is bothering you. And here's a tip: Use a pedometer and measure your steps and you are likely to walk farther.

During the day, look for other ways to be more active and don't forget to make good food choices, and you will be on the road of being more confident, happier, and in better health.

Last night, I tiptoed into Sophia's room to get another glimpse of her sweet face while she was asleep. To my surprise, she wearily lifted her head, and as her blue eyes opened, she groggily called out, "Mama, mama." She reached for me and I picked her up, sat with her on my lap in the rocking chair by her bed, and gently rocked her back and forth.

As I did so, I remembered how my own mother used to rock me in another rocker long ago, and the stories she told as she held me in the secure warmth of her soft arms. Her love for me, as my love is for my children, was immutable and unchanging,

For the next three days, omit white flour, white sugar, and processed foods from your diet. Instead, choose to eat such foods as 100-percent whole-grain products, plenty of fresh fruit, nuts, fish, chicken, eggs, and lots of veggies. Take note of how you feel. Tip: Think ahead. Spend two or three hours of your weekend to plan meals, grocery shop for nutritious ingredients, and prepare some healthy meal choices for the week. (Before beginning any diet regimen, of course, check with your doctor.)

just as God's love for us is always with us, through changes and challenges, through joys and triumphs.

"Nothing in all creation can separate us from God's love for us in Christ Jesus our Lord," says Romans 8:39 (CEV).

And healthful living is truly a part of what God wants for us, for He cares about how we treat our bodies. In fact, John chapter 2 tells how Jesus compares His body to a temple. Let's take a few minutes to read what else the Bible says about taking care of our health.

"Do you not know that your body is a temple of the Holy Spirit, who is in you, whom you have received from God? You are not your own; you were bought at a price. Therefore honor God with your body" (1 CORINTHIANS 6: 19-20, NIV).

"It is vain for you to rise up early, to sit up late" (PSALM 127:2).

"Wine is a mocker, strong drink is raging: and whosoever is deceived thereby is not wise" (PROVERBS 20:1).

"And God said, 'Behold, I have given you every plant yielding seed that is on the face of all the earth, and every tree with seed in its fruit. You shall have them for food'" (GENESIS 1:29, ESV).

"Beloved, I wish above all things that thou mayest prosper and be in health, even as thy soul prospereth" (3 JOHN 1:2).

The Bible promises, "No good thing will He withhold from them that walk uprightly" (Psalm 84:11). Thus, early each morning when I awaken, and every night after I tuck my daughters into their beds, I thank the Creator for His generosity. God is truly the giver of all that is good. At this moment, I'd like you to pause and do the same, saying, "Thank you, God, for your goodness."

What the future holds, I do not know, but one thing is for certain: I am glad God gave me the strength to change what I was yesterday into what I have become today . . . and with His grace, I am eager to see what I can develop into tomorrow.

As you begin to live in the excitement of newfound confidence, you, too, will begin to welcome change as a friend, knowing that God is now, as He has always been, in complete control of His universe and of us, the children who live within it.

WINDOW TWO

HAVE PATIENCE AND AWAIT GOD'S DIRECTION

"Have patience with all things, but chiefly have patience with yourself. Do not lose courage in considering your own imperfections but instantly set about remedying them—every day begin the task anew."

SAINT FRANCIS DE SALES

DAY ONE:

WHEN GOD SAYS, "WAIT," WAIT.

"Be still and know that I am God."
PSALM 46:10, ESV

Are you agonizing and wondering when your situation is going to change?

Have you shed tears and found yourself questioning whether or not God has heard your cries?

Regardless of the situation that confronts you now, your labor is not in vain. The tears that have fallen from your eyes haven't gone unnoticed. And your options have not been exhausted. Brighter days are to come; there is hope for your future. So do not disdain hope. Stay the course. And, with patience, "wait."

It was a beautiful, warm, sunny morning, when a group of fishermen navigated their boat to their favorite spot on the water to spend a productive, yet relaxing day fishing in the deep blue ocean. The fishermen had been to this prime location many times before; for at this particular place, they always seemed to catch an abundance of large fish.

Hours passed, and the fishing trip was indeed successful, as buckets of fish were caught. But suddenly, a vicious storm moved in, and the fishermen found themselves surrounded by a thick, dense fog. Thus, they could only see a few feet in front of them. In an attempt to quickly get back to the safety of the harbor, the fishermen determined which way to steer the boat and then began going in that direction. However, one of them reached in his pocket for a small compass, looked at it, and saw that the dial pointed the opposite way.

Should the fishermen follow their own course? Or should they keep to the directive of the compass? They all agreed to follow the direction of the compass and turn the boat around.

Awhile later, through the fog the fishermen saw the faint silhouette of the shoreline. And they were thankful that the reliable compass had directed them aright. The fishermen had trusted the compass's route, and they returned to the dock safely.

Are you awaiting direction from God and wondering if it will ever come? Are you mired in cares and concerns today? Just as the compass directed the fishermen to safety, in His good and perfect time, God will provide the best course for you.

Imagine that God is walking before you and showing you the way, closing the wrong doors and opening the right windows.

Sometimes, God's direction indicates for you to stay exactly where you are right now. I mentioned in the last chapter how, for a few years, I was in limbo as to my next career move. Being a go-getter, and a career-minded person, it was, at times, frustrating for me to be in this uncertain state. But now I see that my delay in having a clear career direction was directly related to my having more quality time with my children. Hence, the Lord knew best after all. And He often answers our prayers in ways that we cannot comprehend.

Scripture tells us in the Old Testament that God promised Sarah that she would have a baby. Sarah thought she was too old to conceive, because she was 90 years old (well beyond childbearing years), and Abraham was 100. But God said to them, "Is there anything too difficult for the Lord? At the appointed time I will return to you, at this time next year, and Sarah will have a son." And as promised, Sarah did give birth to a miracle son, who they named Isaac (Genesis 18:14, NASB).

So, if you are dismayed, ask yourself, "Is there anything too difficult for the Lord?" With God, nothing can stand between you and your miracle! Remember, we can only do so much, but God can do the impossible. So, let's pray and cast our burdens on Him, and let go of fearful concern over uncertainties that lie ahead. We must practice patience, for He is working on our behalf.

The word *patience* is defined in the *American Heritage Dictionary* as the capacity of calm endurance. As you wait, be attentive to the way in which God will guide you, for it can take on many forms:

✧ Pick up the Bible and read the Psalms and Proverbs, as God leads through His word.

✧ Spend a few minutes a day in complete silence and listen— God speaks through your consciousness, nudging you toward a particular path.

✧ Be alert to the encouragement and wisdom you receive from family, faithful friends, mentors, and even strangers.

✧ When you pray, ask God to show you how you can be effective in each area of your life, and then follow His guidance.

✧ Be on the lookout—He can help you via what may seem like only coincidence.

God will provide direction for us, if we simply trust and wait upon Him.

I am reminded of an astonishing letter I received from a dear reader who wrote, "A few months ago, I was separated from my husband after 32 years of marriage. It has been an extremely difficult period for me and at times I still wonder if this situation is really happening."

Her correspondence continued, "I 'stumbled' across one of your articles about six weeks ago. 'Stumbled' is another word for what I know was 'Divine Intervention' since this was the first time I had ever seen one of your writings.

It was as if you were talking to me directly and knew everything I had been experiencing. [That first] article, and all those that followed, have given me such strength and hope for the future. I have cut out every one, read and re-read them every day. I just wanted to let you know how much you have helped me. I am looking forward to a new chapter in my life with excited anticipation. It will be far from easy, but I know God is close at hand to help me along."

British poet Samuel Taylor Coleridge once wrote, "Chance is but the pseudonym of God for those particular cases which he does not choose to subscribe openly with his sign-manual." Each coincidence is a plan from God telling us that He is in the center of everything that we do. He loves us and watches over every detail of our lives.

I think about the sweet dog that a dear friend of mine, Ginger, adopted from New Orleans, after Hurricane Katrina. In an instant, the dog went from being alone and stranded to being safe and secure, with a family who loves and takes care of him.

It is the same with God, our Father. You may feel alone and stranded, but He can fill the emptiness and heal the hurt. He doesn't leave you in times of trouble. For at this moment, His arms are around your shoulders, patiently leading, strengthening and guiding, walking forward with you down the path of peace.

Feel His love, for it will never fail you.

Day two:

Put aside all anxious thoughts and pray.

"The Lord is good unto them that wait for Him, to the soul that seeketh Him."

Lamentations 3:25

How many hours do you spend worrying?

Have you wasted days fretting over fears and filled with anxieties?

Do you worry about tomorrow? God says, "Therefore do not worry about tomorrow, for tomorrow will worry about itself . . . " (Matthew 6:34, NIV).

Do you worry about situations that you may be confronted with in life? God says, "Never will I leave you. Never will I forsake you" (Hebrews 13:5, NIV).

Do you worry about your future finances? God says, "[I] will supply all your needs . . . " (Philippians 4:19, NASB).

Do you worry when people try to deceive you? God says, "No weapon formed against you shall prosper" (Isaiah 54:17, NKJV).

Do you worry and worry over circumstances that are out of your control? God says, "Do not be anxious about anything, but in everything, by prayer and petition, with thanksgiving, present your requests to God" (Philippians 4:6).

I once heard about a woman who was a chronic worrier and had an idea: for one full year, she decided to keep a record of her worries. Each day, if a worry plagued her, she would write it on her "worry list." As you can imagine, as the months marched on, her list became quite lengthy.

After 365 days, these were her findings: Most of her worries were about circumstances that never happened. Some of her anxieties were related to past regrets and decisions that couldn't be changed. A few of her worries were manufactured in her own mind, while some of her uncertainties had to do with negativity from others. The conclusion? There were legitimate reasons for only five percent of her worries.

After this experiment, the woman realized that daily worrying didn't get her anywhere. As a result, she decided to adjust her thoughts and her attitude, living moment-to-moment, and concerning herself with the 24 hours that were stretched out before her. As this woman stopped worrying about her "past history" and what "might happen" in her future, she found that her mind was no longer clouded or distracted. Thus, each day she accomplished more.

On a weekly basis, write down your worries in a personal calendar. At the end of the week, refer back and see how many of the things you worried about actually happened. You'll be reminded that most of the things you worry about do not come to pass.

One way to crowd out worry is to convert "worry-time" into "prayer-time." If you are tempted to be concerned about a situation, say a prayer, for it has a calming effect and can drive away worry.

You can't pray and worry at the same time.

Penny Martin, president of Holy Land Stone Company, located in Florida, had placed an order for stone to be delivered in November. However, in early August she received a call that the stone was already in the port and would be delivered as soon as her company sent a check for $18,000. August was a very slow month for her company and their cash flow status was not at its best. Thus, she was uncertain as to how they would pay that large sum.

Penny and her office team gather several times a week to pray for the business, their customers, personal intentions, and our world in general. So with no financial solution in sight, Penny gathered the team and prayed, "Father, $18K is nothing to you, but to us right now it is totally impossible. Nothing is impossible for You—for You can do all things! This is Your company, and we trust in You. We thank you and praise You for providing us with this need."

Penny explained to me that a month earlier, she had been contacted by a long-term care organization that wanted to purchase her company's Comfort Crosses™. They had agreed they would prepay 50 percent of their invoice and the balance would be due in 30 days from the date of the invoice.

Most remarkably, a few hours after their prayer, they received a call from the purchasing agent of that long-term care organization. She said she had 54 purchase orders and checks from 54 different facilities that she would overnight to them. Rather than cutting 54 checks up front and then 54 again in 30 days, the purchasing agent decided it would be best to pay it all up front. At that time, Penny had no idea of the quantities they would need, but assumed the sale might be a few thousand dollars. She was thrilled and grateful. That would definitely help pay for the stone! However, not only is God our hope and our trust, but He is also precise. Penny received the package of 54 purchase orders and 54 checks, totaling $18,460!

"Every evening I turn my worries over to God.
He's going to be up all night anyway."

MARY C. CROWLEY

As you patiently wait for God's direction, draw near to Him through prayer. He will draw near to you, and His peace will rule within your heart. Talk to God all day long with these suggestions:

✧ Pray as you are in the car driving to work or running errands.

✧ Call upon God even as you are taking a morning walk.

✧ Pick up the phone, call a friend, and pray together.

✧ Tell God what's on your mind, as you are doing housework.

✧ Say grace before every meal.

✧ Start a prayer group.

While driving to my daughter's softball game at a nearby field, I passed by a house and saw a variety of household items scattered all over their front lawn. "This must be a tag sale," I thought to myself as the car in front of mine slowed down to get a look. Next, I noticed a large sign in front of the house that read, "It's Free!"

That is what our heavenly Father is saying to us: "Come to Me, dear child. Let Me handle your worries, and the price? It's Free!" So, take to God everything that concerns you. His grace and power are far greater than we can imagine, and He stands ready to perform miracles beyond our comprehension. Whatever you need today, God is there for you.

DAY THREE:

THE SECRET OF PATIENCE IS DOING SOMETHING ELSE IN THE MEANTIME.

"Therefore will the Lord wait, that He may be gracious unto you, and therefore will He be exalted, that He may have mercy upon you: for the Lord is a God of judgment: blessed are all they that wait for Him."

ISAIAH 30:18

Through my newspaper column, I had the honor to become acquainted with an exceptional artist named Marcus Hamilton who had enjoyed a 20-year career working in commercial art, doing exquisite hand-drawn illustrations for advertisements, magazines, and book covers. He was a versatile, adaptable artist—supremely gifted, with remarkable creativity and vision.

However, with technical advancements and the emergence of computer-aided graphics, Hamilton's freelance business had slowed down and was running dry. It was difficult for him to find work, and at 50 years old, I'm sure bitter, disparaging thoughts went through this artist's mind. Conceivably, he might have uttered to himself, "My career is finished," "I'm over the hill," and "It's too late for me now to accomplish my dreams." But age is not a factor in God's realm of possibilities or His grand plan for us.

So, having a family to support, Hamilton took a minimum-wage job at a retail department store, and with patience and faith, he remained open to all possibilities. A year later, he was watching a television talk show and, because he was on the lookout for new ideas and opportunities, an interview caught his attention. Cartoonist Hank Ketcham, creator of the beloved cartoon "Dennis the Menace," revealed that he would soon like to retire.

Although Hamilton had never worked as a cartoonist, he boldly called Ketcham and offered himself for consideration to draw Dennis. Ketcham granted him a meeting. Potentially hundreds of thousands of people had watched that television interview, but Hamilton was the only person who had daringly followed through.

When the two artists met, a bond was formed. Ketcham was impressed with Hamilton's striking illustrations, and he admired his creative ideas and persistence. Hence, the two men began working together on comic strip panels for "Dennis the Menace," with Ketcham meticulously imparting his techniques to Hamilton.

In 1995, Marcus Hamilton was given the chance of a lifetime! He joyfully took over the "Dennis the Menace" cartoon illustrations, creating a new comic strip panel each day, thus accelerating his career way ahead. And today, "Dennis the Menace" is entertaining generations of readers around the world, as it is syndicated in more than 1,000 newspapers, in 48 countries, and is translated into over 19 languages.

Hamilton likely had some dire thoughts when his career seemed to be quickly coming to a close, but he managed to remain open enough to possibilities to take bold action when a positive opportunity presented itself. Have you ever had defeatist, pessimistic thoughts? And how can you get your mind off of negative clutter, while you patiently wait for what God has next for you?

Here is the secret: like Hamilton, as you are waiting for situations to work themselves out, *do something else in the meantime.* Occupy yourself with an exhilarating project. Form some new relationships. Be on the lookout for an innovative idea. What I am asking you to do is to participate in a few great pastimes that you can do now which can lead you in the right direction:

- ✧ Get involved with your local church and its activities.
- ✧ Volunteer at a nearby hospital.
- ✧ Help out at your child's or grandchild's school.
- ✧ Join local groups with which you have something in common.
- ✧ Travel to visit family or friends who you haven't seen in a while.
- ✧ Do something that involves using your hands like knitting, scrapbooking, or gardening.
- ✧ Take exercise classes.

One Connecticut reader wrote to me and said, "I have been running daily for 35 years and I am not sure if I could have made it through my difficulties without it." A woman in my hometown once told me that she passes the time during her medical treatments by bringing a canvas and some paints to a destination near her shoreline apartment, where she relaxes by painting the beautiful scenery. Bit by bit, with each brushstroke, her design starts to materialize. And she says that when she sees her picture beautifully coming together, she is reminded that with patience, day by day, her complete health will come together, too. A neighbor and his wife, who are waiting for a possible job transfer to another state, say that they love to take drives in the country on the weekends and browse through antique shops, for they come home feeling refreshed.

Keep active. Talk to people. Browse the newspaper and the Internet for prospects. Do not allow temporary hardships to dim your joy, for crushing disappointments can be camouflaged as wonderful blessings. Soon, like Marcus Hamilton, you will be guided unawares on to something far greater than what came before.

> *"All that I have seen teaches me to trust*
> *the Creator for all I have not seen."*
>
> RALPH WALDO EMERSON

With patience, an impossible dream can become a splendid reality. Thus, don't allow doubts, failures, or past rejections to stop you now. You have so much going for you. God knows your potential. Be patient, it's not too late. Right now, you can be standing in front of a window that will open and reveal a huge blessing.

Therefore, while you are waiting, *do something else in the meantime.* And, as in Marcus Hamilton's story, all it takes is one God-given idea, one phone call, one good break, or one fortuitous meeting for your circumstances to completely turn around and usher you on to the greatest opportunity of your life.

> *"He who can have patience can have what he will."*
>
> BENJAMIN FRANKLIN

And please do not despair if God tarries in His direction for you. Continue to wait on Him to work on your behalf, being assured in the goodness of the outcome. Hark back to the many miracles Jesus performed during the course of His three-year ministry, showing His great love and compassion for people, those who patiently awaited on God.

* Matthew 9:27-29 reveals how Jesus healed two blind men, and in a second their lives were forever changed.
* Matthew 8:23-27, Mark 4:35-41, and Luke 8:22-25 all tell us how Jesus got into a boat with His disciples to cross the Sea of Galilee, and a great windstorm arose when they were far from

shore. Jesus rebuked the wind, saying, "Peace! Be still!" Thus, when the storms of life come against us, at times, we too need to "be still" and "at peace," until the storm passes.

✧ In Luke 5:3-10, Jesus asked Simon to push their boat out a little into the water, and let down his nets. Soon, the nets were so full of fish, they began to tear. This reveals that God can give us abundantly more than we can ask or think of.

✧ And I love Matthew 8:1-5, where Jesus came down the hillside and a leper approached Him, pleading, "If You want to, You can heal me." The man was made well, showing that Jesus wants to help us and give us the desires of our hearts.

God does things in such an amazing way that before long you will look back on how beautifully He orchestrated confusing situations, and you'll say with wonder, "That's something only God could have done!"

God is with you in all that you do. He can make the wrongs come out right. So, "Be truly glad. There is wonderful joy ahead!" (1 Peter 1:6, NLT).

Like a seed that is planted underground, God keeps certain blessings a secret until the precise time comes for Him to send them. And similar to that seed, that blessing, though hidden, is taking root, preparing for a grand and glorious harvest later.

DAY FOUR:

REMEMBER THAT DIFFICULT TIMES, TOO, SHALL PASS.

"I am the vine, ye are the branches: He that abideth in me, and I in him, the same bringeth forth much fruit: for without me ye can do nothing."

JOHN 15:5

You're frustrated, upset.

Tossing and turning. Praying and wondering.

You might let out a deep breath and ask, "What is going on? Where are you, God?"

Maybe you are faced with more than one difficult circumstance and don't understand why "bad things" seem to be continually happening. Perhaps someone insulted you, and you did nothing to deserve the verbal bashing. Or everything you have attempted to do has seemed to go terribly wrong.

Our journey through life is always filled with unexpected challenges. The path is never easy. The climb can be rugged. And now and then, we all encounter struggles.

But, I am asking you to not give way to discouragement and anxiety. Refuse to let negative thoughts or offenses committed against you play over and over, taking up space in your mind. And do not allow unforeseen circumstances that are out of your control to determine your level of joy for the day and or distract you from your great plans for the future.

With God, all things are possible, even at a moment in time when your hopes and dreams for your life seem distant. I think of Daniel in the Bible, a great man of patience, faith, and prayer. The Lord did not prevent the wicked plotting of his adversaries, as Daniel was thrown into a den of hungry lions. Yet, at all costs, Daniel kept his trust in, and loyalty to, God, and God sent an angel to protect him all through the night. In the morning, the King came to the den and called out to him, wondering if he was alive. Daniel answered Him, saying "My God hath sent his angel, and hath shut the lions' mouths, that they have not hurt me" (Daniel 6:22).

Keep in mind that your present condition is not permanent. This season of affliction is temporary. Setbacks are surmountable. And your problems will be resolved successfully, according to God's best plan for you.

Think of yourself standing in front of a large picture window that has outside of it several gifts from God: "New Blessings," "New Opportunities," and "New Joys." All you need to do is have a little more patience, for the window will open shortly and reveal something wonderful.

You will get through these times, as a whole new, splendid life lies before you. God's unendingly gracious Hand will work your situation out, even better than you can ever conceive.

"Patience is the companion of wisdom."

SAINT AUGUSTINE

To feel more empowered, I want you to look away from your difficulty for a little while: slow down, spend 30 minutes listening to spiritual music, sit under a sheltering tree and read an inspirational book, go for an hour-long walk in the sunshine, take a drive in the country, or visit some art galleries. Spend time with children, for you can learn patience from them. Reorganize your home or clean out your closets to conquer clutter and gain more control over your life. When things are in order at home you can feel more creative.

The key: when you take your focus off of the problem and on to a pleasing activity; you'll notice that the problem will appear less formidable. Try planting some flowers or a vegetable garden. Gardening can teach patience and trust, and help you on your journey toward peace. Lori, a longtime friend of mine, explained to me that she finds gardening very therapeutic. Planting seeds, and waiting for them to flower in their own time, helps Lori to be patient with her own dreams that she hopes will eventually transpire. Just as there are seasons for planting and growing, there are seasons in all of our lives. Nature does not hurry. It grows at its own pace.

"Adopt the pace of nature, her secret is patience."

RALPH WALDO EMERSON

So if you're in a slow spell, do as the gardener does and wait with expectation. Although storms may come, the gardener continues to plan and prepare for the harvest. The gardener knows that positive expectation, patience, and preparation lead to success. For the longer it takes, the bigger the harvest.

At work one day, I was talking to a colleague of mine who, years before, had gone through a tough divorce. She shared with me how her abusive ex-husband had left her and her two young children with a house almost in foreclosure, thousands of dollars of debt, and no insurance. And, she was only earning a small amount of money at her part-time job. Certainly, it was the most difficult time in her life.

Looking at my kind, giving, and composed colleague, who today has a happy marriage, well-adjusted children, a lovely home, and a successful career, it was hard to imagine that she had encountered such hard times. "How did you get through that season in your life?" I inquired.

She was silent for a moment. Then, she leaned toward me, as if she were telling me a secret, and said, "When I was in the pool of self-pity and disturbing images entered my mind, trying to consume me, I'd take my mind off the negativity, by reading an old poem that my grandmother once gave to me."

Inquisitively, I asked, "What was the poem?"

She smiled and said, "It is titled: *'This too shall pass.'*"

Summoning me to her office, she beckoned me to follow her down the narrow hallway, and then inside. There, she reached for a frame that sat on her mahogany desk, and gently handed it to me.

I read the encouraging poem, written by Helen Steiner Rice:

If I can endure for this minute
Whatever is happening to me,
No matter how heavy my heart is
Or how dark the moment may be—

If I can remain calm and quiet
With all the world crashing about me,
Secure in the knowledge God loves me
When everyone else seems to doubt me—

If I can but keep on believing
What I know in my heart to be true,
That darkness will fade with the morning
And that this will pass away, too—

Then nothing in life can defeat me
For as long as this knowledge remains
I can suffer whatever is happening
For I know God will break all of the chains

That are binding me tight in the darkness
And trying to fill me with fear—
For there is no night without dawning
And I know that my morning is near.

**Do your dreams seem impossible? A patient person does
not easily give up, for they know that the impossible may
take a little longer to achieve.**

After I silently read the verses, I glanced up at my colleague,
and she confided, "I clung to those words for comfort in the weeks
and months that followed my divorce. This too shall pass, I told
myself. Then, I tried not to allow the bitterness I felt to weigh
me down. Instead, I trusted and believed that God still had great

things to come for us. And diligently, I worked to make a better life for me and my children. Indeed, in His timing, God took care of my situation and turned it around."

Like my colleague, we must run our race through each twist and turn, and remember that the One who created the heavens and earth is still in control. God's eye is watching even the tiniest sparrow, so surely He will take care of us and supply our needs.

DAY FIVE:

GOD HAS A SPECIAL TIMETABLE FOR HIS PLANS TO MANIFEST.

"I will instruct thee and teach thee in the way which thou shalt go: I will guide thee with mine eye."

PSALM 32:8

A mother and father decided to take their six-year-old daughter to the store on her birthday and allow her to choose her own special gift. "You can pick out one present," the mother said to the little girl. Though, in the back of their minds, the parents had a good idea as to what they'd like for their daughter.

So they drove to the mall and, hand in hand, with the child between them, they walked into the department store. One of the first displays that the girl saw was a shelf full of candy. Picking up a bar of chocolate, she exclaimed, "I want candy, Mommy!" The mother responded, "Honey, let's look around the store, and see what else we can find." A bit somberly, her daughter nodded in agreement.

Next, they strolled through the garden center. Quickly, the little girl lifted up a bucket of sidewalk chalk and inquired, "Can I have this for my birthday?"

The father shook his head. "Let's keep looking . . ." he encouraged.

After that, they found their way to the toy department and the girl swiftly reached for a jump rope. "Can I have this?" she asked.

"We should keep looking around just a little more," replied the father. With a sad expression on her face, the girl was beginning to get discouraged. But they continued to shop, browsing up and down each aisle of the store.

Unexpectedly, the little girl spotted an adorable pink and white wooden dollhouse. It was of heirloom quality, and she would be able to treasure and play with it for years to come. The parents watched as their daughter pointed to the dollhouse in awe, not saying a word. So the mother bent down. "Honey, how would you like to have this dollhouse for your birthday?" she whispered.

The little girl was beaming and she cried out, "Yes! I love it!"

All along, the mother and father had intended to buy the dollhouse for their daughter. The child thought a chocolate bar or sidewalk chalk would be okay; however, her parents had something significantly better in mind. There was a purpose behind the shopping trip. And the birthday girl left the department store that day with *far more* than she had anticipated.

Just as these parents had a wonderful birthday gift in mind for their daughter, *God has something marvelous in store for you*, too. God often acts in our lives without our being aware. So, be patient, resolute, and disciplined . . . and refuse to settle for less than God's best plan for you!

> ## *"Wait on the Lord and keep His way, and He shall exalt you to inherit the land."*
>
> PSALM 37:34, NKJV

Beginning in Genesis, 25:29, the Bible recounts the lives of Isaac's two sons, Esau and Jacob. Esau was the firstborn, and in those days, the family name, spiritual position, and a double portion of the inheritance belonged to the eldest son. It was called the "birthright," and it was a sacred blessing.

In spite of this tremendous gift, Esau did not appreciate the value of his birthright and he sold it to his brother Jacob for a pot of stew.

Once when Jacob was cooking some stew, Esau came in from the open country, famished. He said to Jacob, "Quick, let me have some of that red stew! I am famished!" (That is why he was also called Edom.)

Jacob replied, "First sell me your birthright."

"Look, I am about to die," Esau said, "What good is the birthright to me?"

But Jacob said, "Swear to me first." So he swore an oath to him, selling his birthright to Jacob. Then Jacob gave Esau some bread and some lentil stew. He ate and drank, and then got up and left" (Genesis 25:29-34a, NIV).

Do you remember what the spider said to the fly? Paraphrasing from the poem by Mary Howitt: "Oh, wonderful fly, do come into my house. It will be an honor to have you. You are so beautiful," said the cunning spider. And with that one step in the spider's direction, the fly was stuck. It is the same thing when we foolishly rush headlong into things without thinking. Let's heed the old Indian proverb that says, "Take one step; look ten times."

Do you sell yourself short, because you don't wait for God's direction? When you encounter a delay, do you get frustrated and quit? Or, do you rush hastily into situations that are not in your best interest, instead of waiting for God's timing?

Maybe you have not seen a "season" in your life like this before. Perhaps you're lonely, downtrodden, or have experienced a loss. Yet, please do not be tempted or manipulated, like Esau, to give up your "birthright."

Press the "pause" button before you take action toward a particular path and inquire: "Is this the best choice for me?" "Will this decision make me happy?" "Will this choice bring me closer to my ultimate goal?"

I'm asking you to remember your worth. Here is an idea to try: As you wait, put yourself in the presence of excellence:

1. Walk through outstanding architecture, grand hotels, or magnificent churches, and think about the masters who designed these structures. Being in the presence of creative genius can move you to take action to accomplish feats of greatness.
2. Go to the library and feel inspired by the authors and books that surround you. An abundance of creativity is there, which can urge you to go further on your chosen path.
3. Purchase tickets to a musical, theater, or dance performance. Watching the artists' talents can be a powerful energizer, spurring you on to reach for the best in your life.

4. Look for excellence in those around you, and become inspired by them. Realize that the possibilities for your future are plentiful.

You are an heir, a son or daughter of God. And you were created in His image. Your life matters. No one can ever take your place. You're special and extremely gifted, with so much potential. Thus, don't settle or toss away your precious dreams and aspirations because of a setback, conniving person, or temporary problem. Be patient. God has an established plan for your life and a set timetable for these good plans to manifest.

Confucius, the Chinese philosopher, once said, "The most beautiful sight in the world is a little child going confidently down the road after you have shown him the way." Accordingly, if you're lost and need encouragement, allow me to help steer you on the right path by telling you:

✧ Your best opportunities await, if you trust in God.

✧ Don't be distracted or stop now.

✧ You're getting closer to achieving your heart's dream.

✧ The breakthrough that you've been waiting for will soon come to pass.

✧ It's almost time for you to reap your due reward.

The Bible says, "I have heard thee in a time accepted, and in the day of salvation have I succored thee: behold, *now* is the accepted time; behold, now is the day of salvation . . ." (2 Corinthians 6:2, italics mine). The window is opening. Your time has come to go to the next level of success. The tide of destiny has turned. You have cleared your life of the past—now it is just forward to your wonderful future.

DAY SIX:

CAN'T GO ON? HAVE A LITTLE MORE PATIENCE AND TRY JUST ONCE MORE.

"Wait on the Lord: be of good courage,
and He shall strengthen thine heart: wait, I say, on the Lord."
PSALM 27:14

A few years ago, I was told a story that I have never forgotten. It was about a gentleman who drove a taxi part-time in the summer months to supplement his income. Most often, he drove his passengers to a busy local speedway that was bustling with people.

The taxi driver told me how every time he'd pull up to park his taxi to drop off some passengers, a group of kids would be gathered in front of the building at the entrance of the speedway. At that time, it was customary that when passengers got out of their taxi, they'd often toss a quarter or two to these local kids.

Thinking back, the driver remembered one dark-haired boy in particular, because this boy never stopped trying. Some of the other kids would push him to the side in their attempts to grab that quarter from passengers getting out of their taxis. Yet, this boy never pushed back. In fact, he was quite kind and courteous to the other kids, who would intentionally try to knock him down.

Then, one afternoon, the boy's chance arrived.

"I drove up," the driver uttered, "and all the other kids were gathered by another taxi and didn't notice my vehicle."

Continuing, he said, "The boy saw me and came close to my taxi and his face lit up with a glad smile. However, my passenger got out of the taxi and did not toss him a quarter. Instead, my passenger hurried past the boy and shoved him to the side, and he fell to the ground.

The sympathetic taxi driver quickly parked his taxi and scurried out to try to help the boy, but in the crowd, he was nowhere to be found. "I reached into my pocket and pulled out a twenty-dollar bill, for I wanted to give the boy some money for his great efforts. Yet, by the time I spotted him, he was walking away with his head down in despair. Thereafter, I lost sight of the boy and I never did see him again."

The taxi driver recounted how, in the ensuing time since that day, he'd often thought about that dark-haired boy. And he said, "If only the boy had been a bit more patient and waited around just a little while longer, I would have given him twenty dollars, rather than just a quarter that he was after."

The point of this poignant story is: When your circumstance seems hopeless and you're ready to walk away, that is the time when things are most likely to turn around for you.

"When you get into a tight place, and everything goes against you till it seems as though you couldn't hold on a minute longer, never give up then, for that's just the place and time that the tide'll turn."

HARRIET BEECHER STOWE, OLDTOWN FOLKS

Have you made some wrong choices? Or have you faced unjust situations and pain? If so, you may now be saying, "Nothing good will happen for me at this point in my life."

But before you decide to throw in the towel, let me ask you, "Are you going to let someone who hurt you, or your own past mistakes, take away your bright future?" Regardless of what happened before, let me reassure you that your dreams can still happen. There is always hope and a way out of problems. Things will get better, and the time will come when the pain of today will be a distant memory. Hence, keep praying, keep working, keep striving, and keep reaching for your treasured dreams. Don't forget: On the other side of the closed door is an open window.

An illustration of being patient yet steadfast is displayed in an account within the Bible. There was a woman who, for twelve years, endured much pain and suffering. She had undergone many different treatments for her illness without even a glimmer of healing. Still, she had great faith, so that when she saw Jesus pass through, she believed that "If I just touch his clothes, I will be healed" (Mark 5:28, NIV).

This sickly woman worked her way through the crowds until she came up just behind Jesus. Next, she reached out her hand and touched the edge of His cloak. Immediately, her bleeding stopped.

Jesus asked, "Who touched me?" But no one knew. Then, the woman fell at His feet, telling him why she had touched Him and how she had been instantly restored to health.

I love the words Jesus spoke then: "He said to her, 'Daughter, your faith has made you well; go in peace, and be healed of your disease'" (Mark 5:34, ESV).

"Courage and perseverance have a magical talisman,
before which difficulties disappear and obstacles
vanish into air."

JOHN QUINCY ADAMS, ORATIONS

A few days ago, I read an e-mail from a reader who wrote, "Catherine, I've been meaning to write and thank you so much for your inspiring column. You have helped me, with the grace of God, 'hold on' week by week.

"My husband would read your column and say, 'Catherine is writing for you this week.' You were truly a rock and confirmation of the spirit of faith with your words of wisdom."

This reader went on to describe the very challenging, frustrating circumstances she had been experiencing: trying to juggle taking care of ailing parents and a husband with an illness, and all the while working in a negative and toxic environment. Then, out of the blue, she was told by her company that her longstanding job would soon be eliminated. Confused and frightened, she didn't know what the future would hold. But she prayed for patience and guidance, and trusted in God's wisdom and will.

She wrote, "My prayers to the Lord always came back with His one simple word, 'wait,' which is not always an easy thing to do during trials." However, this reader knew that God could change the most hopeless conditions; that some things just can't be rushed. So she held on, worked with positive expectation, and spoke with confident assurance over her situation, thanking God in advance for the answers and solutions yet to come. Forcing all discouraging thoughts out of her mind, she waited, giving God time to show her what He could do.

In the conclusion of her note, the reader reported that, a few

If you do not yet know what God wants you do, then wait expectantly on Him to open the window.

months later, she was offered another position with her company, which she took. Her new responsibilities are better suited to her, she works with a wonderful team of individuals, she's in much healthier surroundings, and now, with her husband on the road to recovery, she feels renewed!

Create a prayer corner: Dedicate a quiet place in your home solely to your own special use. Fill the space with pillows, battery-operated candles, a pen, a notebook, and your Bible. There, you can go and pray. Scripture says, "Enter into thy closet, and, when thou hast shut thy door, pray to thy Father which is in secret; and thy Father, which seeth in secret, shall reward thee openly" (MATTHEW 6:6).

Thinking about my reader's situation, I strolled outside in the overcast afternoon. And as raindrops began to fall from the heavens, I looked upward at the storm clouds above me and I was reminded of the spiritual hymn "Still," by Hillsong:

When the oceans rise and thunders roar
I will soar with you above the storm
Father, you are king over the flood
I will be still and know you are God.

Wait . . . wait on God. Have faith. He is arranging greater blessings for you today.

Day seven:

Take life the way it comes and you will be truly blessed.

"Therefore turn thou to thy God:
keep mercy and judgment and wait on thy God continually."

Hosea 12:6

One of the most inspiring people I've had the pleasure of knowing is 88 years old today, as I write this passage. When I phoned this dear friend of mine, Ray, this morning to wish him a happy birthday, his wife of 60 years told me he had already read the sports section of the newspaper, eaten breakfast, and worked in the garden, and was now across the street helping a neighbor.

About an hour later, my telephone rang and I heard Ray's cheerful voice. "Happy Birthday!" I exclaimed. And, almost in a whisper, I asked him, "So, what's your secret for being ageless and living such a full and joyful life?"

I listened for Ray's reply with much curiosity and respect, and he eloquently answered, "I thank the Lord, go along . . . and take life the way it comes."

How can we become patient? If we learn to accept "what is" and embrace life "in each present moment," our impatience will often fall away.

After our phone conversation, I thought about the nearly two decades that I had known Ray; and despite all the challenging circumstances he has faced, he is always encouraging, hopeful, and optimistic, embracing life with passion!

Ray's advice of *taking life the way it comes* means maintaining a positive frame of mind during times of difficulty. No matter what transpires, possess a steadfast faith in God and a mental power that will allow you to stand unshaken. Disappointments need not stay with you for long. There is an open window that is leading you to truer happiness and greater fulfillment. "I have learned to be content whatever the circumstances" says Paul in Philippians 4:11 (NIV).

Taking life the way it comes helps you to live in the moment. In spite of what has happened in the past, choose to go forward, trusting that God has awesome things prepared for your future. Thus, "Forget what lies behind . . . struggle for what is ahead" (Philippians 3:13, CEV).

Taking life the way it comes is an attitude that forces you to not continually talk about or mull over problems. God does not deny that troubles will come, but He also says, "The Lord will go ahead of you; yes, the God of Israel will protect you from behind" (Isaiah 52:12, NLT).

Taking life the way it comes allows you to be comfortable

with the person who God made you to be. You have extraordinary abilities and talents, so be disciplined in tapping into and developing those gifts to fulfill your highest potential. So, ". . . Do all that is in your heart, for God is with you" (1 Chronicles 17:2, NASB).

Taking life the way it comes makes you realize that God's timing is not always your timing. Therefore, do not lose heart. Work as you wait, for it takes God time to accomplish the good that He wants to do in your life. Live with joyful expectation and persevere, for before long, what you have been waiting for will materialize. "Things which eye has not seen and ear has not heard, and which have not entered the heart of man, all that God has prepared for those who love Him" (I Corinthians 2:9, NASB). And if we let God be our guide, when He does move us, we will be certain that our direction is the correct one.

I recall how a friend of mine left her profession in the fashion industry to be a stay-at-home mom. But she and her husband discovered that one paycheck would not be enough and she would

Do you have situations in your life that are robbing you of your peace? How many hours do you spend watching, reading, or listening to bad news? Tip: Use the 10-minute rule. Set a timer for 10 minutes a day to establish limits on the "negative news" you absorb. When the alarm goes off, switch your focus to the positive outcomes you truly desire, while centering your attention on enjoying each day of your precious life.

soon have to return to work. Rather than worrying, my friend *took life the way it came* and turned to God for guidance, asking specifically for "a career where she could work from home."

Months passed, and because she wasn't apprehensive, she got a terrific idea, and confidently pursued it. My creative friend did not allow all the negative predictions about a shrinking economy to stop her from going forward with her new business concept, for waiting on God is a matter of continuity. Thus, she remained at peace with her decision and refused to listen to negative news.

My friend's brainchild took time and effort, and there were many ups and downs. Yet, she patiently stuck with it and her dream came to fruition. Now, while her children are at school, she works in her home office manufacturing beauty products. With one innovative idea acted upon, and steadfast focus, the desires of her heart were granted.

Let's wake up every morning and take a few minutes to dwell on all the blessings we have for which to be thankful.

Take stock of all that is right in your life by asking yourself, "What five things am I grateful for today?" List them all. And express gratitude to God for them.

A reader from Pennsylvania wrote to me and shared in her letter that maintaining a positive focus had helped her as she healed from an operation. She described how she had written down in a notebook a list of all the happy things in her life, and how rereading the list had helped emphasize her many blessings, and thus, improved her entire outlook.

There are so many possibilities still in front of you. So, if you are feeling apprehensive, say to yourself, as Ray does: *"I'm taking life as it comes."* Then, dare to believe and trust God to open a window, for He can and He will do great things for you and through you.

WINDOW THREE

FORTIFY YOURSELF WITH COURAGE

"Whatever you do, you need courage. Whatever course you decide upon, there is always someone to tell you that you are wrong. There are always difficulties arising that tempt you to believe your critics are right. To map out a course of action and follow it to an end requires some of the same courage that a soldier needs. Peace has its victories, but it takes brave men and women to win them."

RALPH WALDO EMERSON

Day One:

Confront that giant and you will conquer it.

"Be strong in the Lord and in His mighty power."
EPHESIANS 6:10, NIV

Are you confronting a giant in your life? Are you face-to-face with an enormous obstacle that is incredibly overwhelming?

If so, God is saying to you today,

"Behold, I am the Lord, the God of all flesh.
Is there anything too hard for Me?"

JEREMIAH 32:27, NKJV

The mighty hand of God is never far away. Be courageous; God is with you wherever you go, and He will meet your needs in His time and in His way. So, reflect on these points:

✦ One touch of God's hand of grace can solve your problems.

✦ His power can heal and restore.

✦ And instantly, He can put an idea into your mind that can bring you a unique opportunity and change your life.

Trust in God's positive plan and keep pursuing those high goals confidently. Dream boldly and bravely, and move ahead without fear. God will honor your efforts as long as you keep trying, for He promises victory to those who have the courage and faith to take the first step, despite what giants they may encounter.

A sterling example of courage is portrayed in the life of Caleb. In the Old Testament, the book of Numbers explains that after freeing the people from slavery under Pharaoh, Moses led them, including Caleb, to the edge of the Jordan River toward the land of abundant crops and safety. God delivered His people so that they could enter the land and enjoy the blessings He had prepared for them. Before entering Canaan, though, Moses sent twelve spies to explore the territory to see what they were up against.

When the spies returned, the fearful, negative account from ten of the spies was that the Canaanites were huge, eight-foot giants. Plus, there were locked gates and high walls surrounding the city entrance that were impenetrable.

However, the other two spies, Caleb and Joshua, had different mindsets. They were focused on God, not the giants. And they believed that they should go forward into the land, since God had already promised it to them and urged them to go and take it.

Caleb stilled the people and said, "Let us go up at once, and possess it; for we are well able to overcome it" (Numbers 13:30). God had displayed His power before, and Caleb had faith that God would go before them and help them once again. Regardless of the negative reports, Caleb trusted God and His word. Caleb continued to appeal wholeheartedly, "Do not rebel against the Lord. Do not be afraid of the people of the land. We will swallow them up. The Lord is with us" (14:6-9).

The people were fearful and full of doubt. They didn't believe. Paralyzed by the thought of facing those giants, they decided to turn away, forfeiting their opportunity to go forth into a land "flowing with milk and honey," and thus, they returned to life wandering in the wilderness.

Yet Caleb did not give up on his dream, nor did he ever doubt God's goodness in fulfilling His promise. Years later, God guided the people back to the same river's edge. And with Moses's passing, Joshua led Caleb and the Israelites victoriously across the Jordan River to the Promised Land. Moreover, because of Caleb's faithfulness, all of his descendants also inherited the land.

"Courage is not defined by those who fought and did not fall, but by those who fought, fell, and rose again."

ANONYMOUS

How many of us draw back in fear when challenged with a difficulty? What opportunities do we miss because someone mistreated us or told us "no," or because we made a mistake? Thereafter, we retreat and then convince ourselves that "our dreams are over" and "things will never get better." Sometimes, the negative noise that goes on in our heads can get in the way, the giants reminding us again and again of all the times we've tried and failed, the fears, and the regrets.

What are you afraid of today?

✧ Identify your fears; take honest inventory of them.

✧ Ask yourself, "What are the potential benefits of moving past these fears? Are they worth some risk? What do I have to lose by relinquishing my fears?"

✧ Now, compose a paragraph on how your life would be different if you *overcame* those fears.

✧ Write specific *actions* that you can take now to begin to confront those fears.

✧ Then, take that first step. You build courage by moving forward. Don't hesitate. Act in spite of fears, for every time you face a fear, the next circumstance that comes along in which you are fearful will be easier to handle.

> *"The man who removes a mountain begins*
> *by carrying away small stones."*
>
> CHINESE PROVERB

Do not allow fear, doubt, and disbelief to hold you back anymore. Never let negative opinions cause you to raise the white flag of surrender and recede. Don't turn away and give up, expecting the worst.

One of my business associates' sons wanted to apply to an Ivy League university. Someone made a negative remark to him, stating, "You'll never get into that school. Don't even bother submitting an application." As that unconstructive comment moved through the young man's mind, the determined teenager said to himself, "I am going to try, anyhow, because I believe this is where the Lord wants me." That young man let his faith lead the way. He applied to that Ivy League school and he was accepted with a scholarship. He has now graduated with honors and has a successful career.

Tip: When getting advice, keep three words in mind: Consider the source.

You, too, can draw strength from your faith and refuse to quit! I want you to know that giants cannot defeat you. Stumbling blocks can't keep you down. No one can deprive you of your God-given dreams. Silence the negative voices, and turn in the direction of the positive voice that says, as Caleb declared, "I am well able to overcome," "I will not be afraid," and "The Lord is with me."

Face up to a fear with this technique: Perform an act you fear over and over until it has no more power over you. For instance, if you are afraid of talking to a friend about a certain issue, or you're nervous about making a sales call or asking for help, face your fear, take action, and "just do it." Your courage will grow as you repeat the action each time. Finally, your fear will disappear.

A Virginia reader wrote via e-mail, "Regardless of the questions that go unanswered in our lives, the answer we do have is the one that says that God is always there for us." Hence, let's get past our fears by shifting our eyes off of the "giants" and on to our all-powerful, all-wise, and loving God.

"Be brave . . . have faith! Go forward!"
Thomas Edison

There is nothing too difficult for God; He can do the impossible. Therefore, let us keep hold of our courage and our faith, and continue progressing onward, believing that God will lead us to our promised land. And we will live the extraordinary life God wants us to live!

DAY TWO:

BE DETERMINED TO FOLLOW YOUR HEART AND YOU'LL WIN THE RACE BEFORE YOU.

"David also said to Solomon his son, 'Be strong and courageous, and do the work. Do not be afraid or discouraged, for the Lord God, my God, is with you. He will not fail you or forsake you until all the work for the service of the temple of the Lord is finished.'"

1 CHRONICLES 28:20, NIV

The temperature climbed to over 100 degrees. Outside it was oppressively humid and muggy. But regardless of the weather, day after day, the young athlete kept going, forging on, running extensive distances, her strides long and fast.

She was an Olympic track and field hopeful. And with every step, as she vigorously trained, I can imagine her saying to herself, "I will live up to my full potential; I am going to try my best to win." And then, increasing her pace, pushing as hard as she could, she probably uttered, "I'm not going to allow my past setbacks to ruin my hope for the future."

The athlete progressed forward, sprinting, running, jumping, and squinting into the hot sun. I'm sure tears must have dropped from her eyes and onto the heat of the charcoal-colored pavement as she thought back on her struggles.

Born prematurely in 1940 into a poor family in the South, Wilma Rudolph spent the early years of her life plagued by illnesses. Polio left her partially paralyzed and she was unable to walk without the aid of a metal brace. Because Wilma had physical disabilities, pain, and poverty to reckon with, people most likely thought she wouldn't have much of a future. Yet she refused to give up, and with the help of physical therapy she worked through her countless obstacles.

Wilma did not center her attention on unconstructive predictions or limitations, for innately she must have known how negativity could have intensified their power over her. Instead, with remarkable courage and determination, Wilma focused on her strengths and her dreams and goals.

Ask yourself what Vincent Van Gogh did:
"What would life be if we had no courage to attempt
anything?" Then write down what your heart tells you.

After years of therapy, Wilma removed her leg brace and, little by little, she regained the use of her leg. Thereafter, she desperately wanted to play high school basketball, and she developed into a fine player. As destiny would have it, unexpectedly, Wilma attracted the attention of a college track and field coach. "You have the potential to be a great runner," the coach encouraged her. He knew this talented young lady was a natural athlete, so he asked her high school coach to form a girls' track team. Soon, Wilma began setting records and leading her team to victory.

Then, in 1960, Wilma Rudolph represented the United States in the Olympic Games. Her extraordinary performances made history! Wilma established a world record, as she won three gold medals in track and field and was dubbed one of "the fastest women in the world." Moreover, through her autobiography, television movie, motivational speeches, foundation, and work as a schoolteacher, she imparted the lessons that she had learned to others, making the story of Wilma Rudolph a true inspiration. Her story reminds me of the old poem "Good Timber," by Douglas Malloch, which says, "The stronger the wind, the mightier the oak becomes."

No matter where you were raised, despite disadvantages, disabilities, or lack, like Wilma Rudolph, you, too, can courageously rise above difficulties, to claim a fulfilling life.

The word "courage" comes from the Latin root "cor," which means "heart." For *"heart"* is the root of all courage. Thus, follow your own heart and be true to yourself.

Is there something in your life that you just can't get past? Is it the fear of taking on a new challenge at the risk of possibly failing? Are you afraid of letting go of a comfortable situation that you know is not in your best interest? Are you uncertain about something, not knowing which direction to go?

Here are seven ways to help you gain the courage it takes to follow your heart:

1. Evaluate your strengths. Reflect on everything that you do well: your skills, talents, and positive attributes.
2. Remind yourself daily of your abilities and desires by saying positive affirmations, such as these below, aloud:

✧ I'm strong and capable of achieving my goals.

✧ God is going before me and showing me the way.

✧ I'm a good, kind person.

✧ I am worthy of love, success, and happiness.

✧ My future is bright.

Declare these affirmations several times *out loud*; you can retain twice as much by reciting them aloud rather than silently.

3. Believe in yourself, think positively about what you are going to do, and concentrate on what you'd like to see happen.

4. Create a mental picture as a motivational tool. In your mind's eye, see the possibilities to come; imagine your situation being positively transformed. Build a vision in your heart and work towards it.

Have tunnel vision. Keep your eye on the prize. Don't take your eyes off of your goal for a moment, and believe that it will come to pass.

5. Act with courage and conviction, living that vision *as if* it were already true. Then, take the steps necessary to begin the task.

6. Make reflecting on all the good things that happened during your day a part of your evening routine.

7. Before bedtime, draw courage from God by reading Biblical verses such as:

✧ "He giveth power to the faint, and to them that have no might He increaseth strength" (Isaiah 40:29).

✧ "I can do all things through Christ who strengthens me" (Philippians 4:13, NKJV).

✧ "The name of the Lord is a strong tower; the righteous runs to it and is safe" (Proverbs 18:10, NASB).

✧ "Do you not know that in a race all the runners run, but only one gets the prize? Run in such a way as to get the prize" (2 Corinthians 9:24, NIV).

You're able to go further than you think is possible. Just try. There will be plenty of people who say, "No, it can't be done," but I want you to act anyway. You are capable of more than others deem probable. Keep at it! You can bring about your goals. Thus, set your heart and mind on your achievements and continuously persist. For the hills and valleys that you are passing through are not designed to stop you, but to strengthen you.

"The future belongs to those who believe in the beauty of their dreams."

ELEANOR ROOSEVELT

I am reminded of the life of Job in the Bible. The story goes that Job lost almost everything that was valuable to him. Yet, despite his afflictions, he never lost his faith in, or dependence on, God. And Job 42:12 explains that, "the Lord blessed the latter end of Job *more* than his beginning" (italics mine). In other words, the Lord brought about and gave Job "more" at the end of his life than he had had at the beginning.

Today, please persist with courage and focused determination, moving ahead to the Divine destiny that God has beautifully prepared for you. Keep your eyes on Him. And before you know it, as long as you follow your heart and refuse to give up, you'll triumphantly cross the finish line in first place!

Day three:

Learn from mistakes
and fail forward.

*"Fear not, for I have redeemed you; I have called you by name,
you are mine. When you pass through the waters . . . they shall
not overwhelm you; when you walk through fire you shall not be
burned, and the flame shall not consume you.
For I am the Lord your God."*
Isaiah 43:1-3, ESV

Before practice one afternoon, a college basketball coach gathered
her players together in the gymnasium, and said, "The team that
makes the most mistakes usually is the team who will win." One
student, a bit puzzled, asked, "Coach, what do you mean?"

The coach looked at each team member in the eye, and
declared, "Let me explain . . . It is the *doer*, the *go-getter*, the
positive achiever who makes honest mistakes. Why? Because
mistakes are made from *doing* . . ."

She went on, "In sports, in school, and in life in general, we
must anticipate obstacles. So if you fall down, stand up. Make the
necessary corrections and try again!"

The athletes nodded with understanding. That moment was

a turning point in their lives, when they realized they should not run and hide or feel sorry for themselves or guilty because of an unintentional mistake. Instead, they must have courage and persevere.

Thereafter, enthusiastically, the coach exclaimed, "Success comes when we learn from our mistakes and when we keep on going, and earnestly, honestly keep on *doing!*"

"The majority of men meet with failure because of their lack of persistence in creating new plans to take the place of those which fail."

NAPOLEON HILL

Start by asking yourself today, "What incidences from the past still come into my mind and make me feel unhappy? How do I treat an apparent failure? Do I dwell on it? Does it stop me from opening the window to new beginnings?"

You must allow for errors in yourself and in others, reminding yourself that mistakes are a part of the learning process. Do you take a failure or a setback personally? Well, as an alternative, what if I asked you to view it as a temporary, isolated incident and then optimistically focus on what's to come? Soon, you would uncover the hidden gift that "failure" can bring to you. Try the following:

1. Re-evaluate your priorities.
2. Set new goals, focusing on positive possibilities for the future.
3. Begin a simple undertaking now that you know you can achieve. Accomplishment in each little work can build your courage and lead you onto greater successes.
4. Push through the learning curves, for we learn by trial and error. Every experience will help you gain more useful information, wisdom, and stamina for the next time.

5. Keep in mind that, most often, setbacks are chances to rise up even stronger.

Depending on what you do, failures can be dead ends or learning experiences that can lead you to try other routes to success. Here's a great tip to follow: look at mistakes as "wise teachers" and use them "to make corrective changes," seeking "constructive solutions." In other words, use each mistake to make yourself better. Life will teach the lessons, but it is up to you to learn from them.

I like the story about Arthur Blank and Bernie Marcus, who in 1978 unexpectedly lost their management jobs at a chain of hardware stores. Instead of viewing their job loss as a negative and being overwhelmed with despair, these seasoned business professionals saw this adversity as an opportunity to improve their conditions and take positive control of their future careers.

Receptive to innovation and possessing entrepreneurial spirits, the men had been envisioning, for a while, a new approach to the home-improvement field. As a result, the two men decided to join forces and formulated a plan to implement their vision.

Some critics laughed at them when they heard about their pioneering business idea—a new concept for a nationwide chain of home-improvement stores. Yet, the courageous, strong-willed men did not let other people talk them out of daring to reach for success.

Arthur Blank and Bernie Marcus continued to research their

brainchild: superstores with a wide variety of products at low prices and excellent customer service. They applied their knowledge, and with a positive outlook and a desire to make a difference in the lives of others, enthusiastically worked toward their venture. A year later, Arthur Blank and Bernie Marcus co-founded the Home Depot store chain.

"There is no experience in any life which if rightly recognized, rightly turned and thereby wisely used, cannot be made of value; many times, things thus turned and used can be made sources of inestimable gain: oftentimes, they become veritable blessings in disguise."

RALPH WALDO TRINE

It's been said that life follows thought. The way we approach failures will determine the ultimate outcome. With courage, a mistake can be "a little step back" that may actually bring you "two big steps forward."

Ecclesiastes 3:1 says, "To everything there is a season, and a time to every purpose under the heaven." Let's keep in mind that God's timing is not always our timing. When He gives you a vision for your life, that dream may very well require months or years of working and waiting, with trials and errors, before it comes to fruition.

In the Old Testament of the Bible, there is an example of failing forward in the life of Joseph. When Joseph was a teenager, he had a dream related to his successful future position. Yet, the dream did not come to pass overnight. Joseph went through years of unfair trials and tribulations. The book of Genesis conveys the many difficulties Joseph endured: his brothers conspired against him, cast him into a pit, and then sold him for 20 pieces of silver to slave traders, and, subsequently, while living as a slave, false accusations against Joseph resulted in his imprisonment. But God was always with him. And Joseph understood that patience was needed to allow God to accomplish His purposes. Joseph learned from the past, was faithful and courageous, and did what was right.

God gave Joseph the remarkable gift of translating dreams. While Joseph was in prison, Pharaoh had a dream and called upon Joseph to interpret it. Joseph told Pharaoh that the dream indicated there would be a famine in the land. He advised Pharaoh to store up grain to avoid starvation. And because of this, Joseph saved the lives of many people. Pharaoh was so impressed with Joseph that he placed him in a position of enormous power and responsibility, as the second highest ruler in the Egyptian empire. In God's timing, Joseph's teenage vision was fulfilled, and the rest of his life was blessed.

> *"He fills my life with good things. My*
> *youth is renewed like the eagle's!"*
>
> PSALM 103:5, NLT

My oldest daughter, Lauren, plays the clarinet in the school band. Before her winter concert, I heard melodies coming from her room, as she repeatedly practiced just the last part of a song. I walked upstairs and asked her, "Honey, why are you just practicing the end of that composition?"

She put the clarinet down on her table and said, "I think that the last measures of the music are most important, Mom."

Confused, I questioned, "What makes you think so?"

Wisely, Lauren clarified, "Well, if I make a mistake in the beginning of the performance, the audience will most likely not remember it. So, I have to make the last part of the song *the absolute best.*"

*"Courage is going from failure to failure
without losing enthusiasm."*

WINSTON CHURCHILL

Perhaps your start in life was less than perfect. Or maybe you have stumbled and fallen, failed, and suffered much. Whoever or wherever you are today, I want you to pick yourself up and go on, without wasting a moment in regret. God's love toward you never changes. It's unconditional, and His mercy and grace are always there for you. Let go of emotional wounds, begin again, and be determined to make the next chapter of your life *the absolute best*!

DAY FOUR:

THE SMALL VOICE WITHIN GUIDES YOU TO BIGGER THINGS IN LIFE.

"For the eyes of the Lord are over the righteous and His ears are open unto their prayers . . ."

1 PETER 3:12

Throughout life, God speaks to our conscience, by way of our instincts, "inner voice," and gut feelings, giving to each of us a sense of right and wrong. Oftentimes, by way of our intuition, warning signs and signals are strategically placed in our path. Perhaps we're approaching future danger, and we may sense a "Stop" sign. Or if we are headed off course, we might detect that we're going in "the wrong direction." And possibly we feel uncomfortable as we turn a corner, perceiving a sign that says, "Keep out."

However, when we see these cautionary signs, it is up to us to select the right road on which to journey. Hence, let us be prayerful and sensitive to what is around us. Let us trust and obey those inner resources, the quiet whisper within that leads us to God's peace.

*"Make your ear attentive to wisdom, and
incline your heart to understanding."*

PROVERBS 2:2, NASB

I have heard it said that "Our associations can make or break us." You must discern character and pick your company prudently. Right now, ask yourself some serious questions: "Have I allowed people, with their own issues, to cause me to feel bad about myself?" "Every time I am around (fill in the blank), do they consistently bring me down?" "Does my relationship with (fill in the blank) help me or hurt me?" Have the courage to separate from individuals whose purpose—intentional or unintentional—is not to help, but to hurt. Some people don't intend to hurt but are always doing so anyway and are thus just as unhealthy to be around.

Be cautious of whom you trust, being wise enough to consider others' moral fiber thoroughly before confiding in them. Are you wasting time on relationships that have no "staying power"? Start becoming aware of how you feel after you have interacted with certain people. Are you uplifted and strengthened? Or are you confused and in a worse mood? Those who are constantly negative, with continual bad attitudes and habits, will drag you down. Take notice, heed the warning, and guard against unconstructive influences and unfavorable environments.

You only have one life, so make it one of supreme moral courage. You are too precious to be manipulated and controlled. Distracters can get you off track and keep you from moving forward to achieve your full potential. Thus, if you get an uneasy feeling when you are with someone, listen to that inner resource and "exit."

A courageous young man from California wrote to me and described how he had been struggling with a dependency on drugs.

Although he had enjoyed a great upbringing, wrong associations had contributed to his addictions. First, it was drinking with the crowd, then drugs and pills. Soon, his life was falling apart, and he did not know where to turn.

Thankfully, he began rehabilitation, and he explained how the Lord had filled his life with hopes and aspirations. He had listened to the inner promptings of his heart, was pulled out of the bondage of his addiction and suffering, and was saved by God's grace. "Even when I felt like giving up," he wrote, "God did not give up on me." Today, this young man is free of his addictions. He has made new friends, and he's a counselor, helping others who are going in situations similar to the one he was in.

> *"The ultimate measure of a man is not where he stands*
> *in moments of comfort and convenience, but where*
> *he stands at times of challenge and controversy."*
>
> MARTIN LUTHER KING, JR., STRENGTH TO LOVE

Remain determined to not let anything keep you from God's best plan for your life. Ask yourself, "What are the principles upon which my life is built?" Jot down those principles in a daybook, and live those good values. Travel the high road, stand upright, and continue being a person of honor and excellence.

A great example of integrity comes from a story about young Theodore Roosevelt. In his early years as a rancher out West, Roosevelt and some of his ranch hands were rounding up stray cattle. It is purported that one of the hands wandered onto a neighbor's property, where he found an unbranded calf. By Western tradition, the calf belonged to the neighbor. But the ranch hand started to tie up the calf and put the Roosevelt brand on it.

Roosevelt saw what this hand was doing and asked him, "Why are you doing that?" The worker replied, "It's gonna be your calf, boss." Incensed, Roosevelt said to the man immediately, "You're fired. A man who will steal for me will steal from me."

Make today the day of decision. From this moment forward, walk through every minute taking a stand for what is right. Do not be satisfied with just casual standards. Go the extra mile and make good choices. Courage is always doing the right thing.

✦ Live by a code of super-honesty.

✦ Be true to your word.

✦ Say what you mean and mean what you say.

✦ Have the courage to say "No."

✦ Stand up for what is truth.

✦ If a mistake was made in the past, say, "I'm sorry," ask for forgiveness, repent, and let it go.

✦ Adhere to straight moral values.

Create a stronger self through personal integrity. When faced with a decision or problem, take a walk outdoors and search your heart for answers. Before proceeding, ask yourself, "Is this the right thing to do?" and follow what your heart says.

Do you remember the story of the Prodigal Son in the Bible? A father had two sons, and the younger son asked his father to give him his portion of his inheritance from the family estate early. The father granted his request and the young son set off to distant lands and began to waste his fortune in debauchery. A famine hit the country, the young son's money ran out, and he found himself destitute, in horrible conditions. Finally, the young son came to his senses and returned home. Upon seeing his beloved son, the father, who had been watching and waiting for him, ran out to greet him with open arms and rejoiced that his son had found his way back home (Luke 15:11-32).

Perhaps you've had some difficult times. Possibly you engaged in some poor choices in the past. Or maybe you made one particular bad decision about a certain significant direction. But it is never too late to ask for mercy, to turn your back on past mistakes and begin anew. And as the Bible story illustrates, your Father in heaven will welcome you with open arms and rejoice when you find your way back home.

There is only one of you. Never let anyone or anything steal your self-worth, your dreams, or your God-inspired aspirations. Listen to that still, small voice. And trust and seek God. He will guide your path and even "the wrath of man" (Psalm 76:10) shall be invariably turned to your advantage.

As you travel on the road of life, pay attention to your conscience. Remain sensitive to God's voice. For the signs that God has for you read:

"Nothing will be impossible for you"
(MATTHEW 17:20, NIV).

"For God has not given you a spirit of fear and timidity, but of power, love, and self-discipline"

(2 TIMOTHY 1:7, NLT).

"I will restore you to health and heal your wounds"

(JEREMIAH 30:17, NIV).

"I am with you always"

(MATTHEW 28:20, NIV).

You have not seen anything yet. Your day of victory is at hand. Have the faith to believe it's possible, and you'll be amazed at what God will do for you.

DAY FIVE:

DEFEAT MAY TEST YOU, BUT IT DOESN'T HAVE TO STOP YOU.

"Immediately he spoke to them and said, 'Take courage! It is I. Don't be afraid.' Then he climbed into the boat with them, and the wind died down. They were completely amazed."
MARK 6:50-51, NIV

At one time, I was tempted to give up on a goal that I knew could potentially help millions of people. I experienced months and months of opposition and I wondered if this was truly where God wanted me. "Maybe I should recede?" I questioned.

Searching for an answer, I was led to seek advice from a wise woman with whom I was acquainted. Now in her 80s, I have known her for years and respect her opinion. So we made plans for an early afternoon tea and as I strolled up her cobblestone walkway, her sweet home and manicured landscape reminded me of a Norman Rockwell painting.

She welcomed me with a warm embrace and said kindly, "Sit down, dear, and tell me what is troubling you."

Sitting comfortably in a soft, brown chair, I took a deep breath and proceeded to explain to her my ongoing dilemma. "Should

I continue?" "Do I have the strength to carry on with this new venture?" and "Is this God's will for me?" I asked.

And I whispered, "Something is hindering my progress."

She listened with an understanding, sympathetic ear. Then, without saying a word, she stood up and disappeared into the next room. A minute later, she returned, holding something in her hand.

"Catherine, my dear one," she tenderly uttered, "I know what is holding you back."

With a look of surprise, I inquired, "You do?"

"Yes," she said knowingly.

After that, she handed me a shiny silver compact.

"What's this?" I asked, as I reached out my hand to clutch it. I held the pocket-sized compact for a moment, a bit confused.

"Open it," she urged.

With a puzzled look on my face, I did as she requested and gingerly opened the compact. All I saw was my reflection in the mirror.

"Look closer," she encouraged.

Neither one of us said a word—there was complete silence. But my heart and soul were touched with pure understanding.

In the round, mirrored compact, I saw the reflection of myself.

The wise woman stated, "There's just one person who is holding you back from being 'you' . . . and that is *you*!"

Astonished, I was stunned to silence, as she continued, "Your situation will change when you change, so don't think you can't . . . because, dear, you can!

"Defeat may test you, but it doesn't have to stop you. All things are possible when you are courageous, have faith in God, have confidence in yourself, and persist for the good of others."

I still smile when I remember that day, for I learned: victory is where you are and within yourself. For even when a person has limited resources, they can find remarkable courage and strength within.

So, *fret not* because "We are more than conquerors through Him who loved us" (Romans 8:37, NIV).

Faint not, since "God is our refuge and strength, an ever-present help in trouble" (Psalm 46:1, NIV).

And, *Fear not,* for "He gives strength to the weary and increases the power of the weak." Then, keep on going forward!

In the Old Testament, the Bible tells how God provided manna (a form of sustenance) for His people while they were in the wilderness during their journey to the Promised Land. Each day, except on the Sabbath, God sent manna. The people were instructed to gather as much as they wanted, for it would never run out. Yet, other than on the day before the Sabbath, the people were not allowed to stock up on the manna; they were to gather just enough for their daily needs. The keynote to this story is that by meeting their needs daily, rather than weeks in advance, God taught His people to trust Him. And as we progress ahead, we should trust God in the same manner.

What past difficulties have inspired you to new achievements? What "blessings in disguise" have transpired in your life? Ponder past situations, personal and professional, that turned around for good, and make note of them in a journal for future reference.

I'm asking you to not continually look back or hang your head in defeat. For the hardships that you face can provide you with a chance to discover who you really are, what you are made of, and what you're destined to become—and a chance to share your success, instead of defeat, with others.

> *"It takes courage to grow up and
> become who you really are."*

E. E. CUMMINGS

Benjamin Franklin was raised in a humble home, with little education or advantages, yet he became a prominent inventor, scientist, author, and statesman. Andrew Jackson was orphaned at age 14 and later was a prisoner of war, but he went on to become the seventh president of the United States. Elizabeth Barrett Browning suffered from an illness that caused her to become an invalid. But even now, she is one of the most respected poets of her era.

Struggles can give you the strength and fortitude you need for future successes. For one of the greatest things about pursuing and achieving goals is surmounting what you've had to endure in order to get there.

Have a heart-to-heart talk with someone you trust. You may discover that they have faced the same issues as you, and thus may be able to share a way through these troubles.

In 1943, the studio of one of my favorite illustrators, Norman Rockwell, was burned down in a fire. All of his cherished paintings, props, sketches, and books were destroyed. Although the fire demolished Rockwell's work, all was not lost. The flames did not destroy his confidence in his extraordinary artistic abilities. So what did he do? Rockwell overcame that misfortune, rebuilt his studio, and courageously started over. Soon, he was illustrating his brilliant masterpieces once again.

"Somehow I can't believe that there are any heights that can't be scaled by a man who knows the secret of making dreams come true. This special secret, it seems to me, can be summarized in four C's. They are Curiosity, Confidence, Courage, and Constancy, and the greatest of all is Confidence. When you believe in a thing, believe in it all the way, implicitly and unquestionably."

WALT DISNEY

Confidence gives you courage to overcome self-defeat. Hence, to develop confidence in yourself, here are eight suggestions:

1. Be aware of your self-talk. When speaking about yourself, speak in positive terms only.
2. Put your best foot forward. Practice good grooming habits. Smile every day to be happy and more confident. Stand up straight, hold your head up, walk tall, and wear clothes that make you feel great.
3. Wear a vibrant color—hot pink, turquoise blue, or royal purple—to alter your mood.
4. Empower yourself by doing something out of your comfort zone. Spend time growing spiritually, attend workshops, or learn something new to increase your knowledge. Action is a key to developing confidence.
5. Surround yourself with positive people. And make eye contact when you are engaged in a conversation.
6. Always look at the bright side of life and appreciate what you have, such as: good health, your family and friends, pets, and a roof over your head.
7. Take care of your health. Eat nutritious foods and get a good night's sleep, even if it means leaving some things undone in

your day. Try taking self-defense, kickboxing, or body-combat classes, as physical fitness has a huge effect on self-confidence.

8. Act in accordance with the "Golden Rule," and shift your attention on to someone else. Concentrate on the personal contributions that you can make to the world, and go out and create them.

A few days ago, I opened a letter from a single mother of seven beautiful children. She told how life has been difficult, but despite the hardships before her, she found the inspiration within herself to write a book. After ten years, she published her first novel, with a successful release event. "God gave me the gift of creativity," she wrote, "and I trust Him."

"Take a chance! All life is a chance. The man who goes farthest is generally the one who is willing to do and dare."

DALE CARNEGIE

Remember, there is only one person holding you back . . . and that is yourself! Boldly go forth, and with God by your side, you can have the courage to persevere. Believe in your ability to succeed, for I believe in you! Nothing can stop you now.

DAY SIX:

THE WORDS YOU SPEAK ARE FULL OF POWER.

"For truly, I say to you, if you have faith like a grain of mustard seed, you will say to this mountain, 'Move from here to there,' and it will move, and nothing will be impossible for you."

MATTHEW 17:20, ESV

Recall in the Bible the story about King Hezekiah. Hezekiah became very sick, and as he lay down, unknowingly, on his deathbed, the Lord sent the prophet Isaiah to tell Hezekiah to put his affairs in order, for the illness would soon take his life.

After Isaiah told Hezekiah the catastrophic news, the king was struck with grief and anguish. Yet, instead of sitting back and accepting this fate, Hezekiah stepped up in faith, turned his head to the wall, and prayed, speaking aloud, reminding the Lord of all the good that he had accomplished in faithfulness in His sight. Hezekiah put action behind his requests. He believed, and tearfully prayed for healing, asking that the Lord restore him back to health.

And almost at once, the Lord answered Hezekiah's plea. Before Isaiah had even left the palace grounds, he went back to see King Hezekiah with a new message: that the Lord had heard his prayers and had seen his tears, and that Hezekiah would indeed recover and would live another 15 years (2 Kings 20:1-11; 2 Chronicles 32:24; Isaiah 38).

What words are you speaking over your situations? Have you ever stopped for a moment and really thought about the words you speak? What do you say concerning your own future? Or, how often do you talk without even realizing the great significance of your words?

Like Hezekiah, let's pray, speaking words of faith, believing, and using what we say to transform our situations. Our words are filled with power. The words that we speak are like a wand that can allow us to alter conditions one way . . . or the other way.

"Thou shalt also decree a thing, and it shall be established
unto thee: and the light shall shine upon thy ways."

JOB 22:28

Whatever we send out, by our thoughts, our words, deeds, and actions, will come back around. Think before you speak. And if someone else is talking badly about another, do this: Change the subject.

Hence, before you say a word about yourself or to others, ponder a few questions: "Who will benefit from what I am about to say? Could somebody's feelings be hurt? If I make a negative comment, could that person's hopes, dreams, or self-esteem become damaged? Is what I am about to say kind? Am I using my words to bless others?"

The following are some suggestions I'd like you to try to incorporate into your day:

✧ Express to your loved ones: "I'm so proud of you," "I love you," "You mean so much to me."

✧ Tell your friends often: "I appreciate you," "You're special," and "Thank you for being there for me."

✧ Cheer the dispirited and say: "My prayers are with you," "Everything is going to be all right," and "I am here if you need help."

✧ On the job: Inject peaceful, calming words into conversations and watch how solutions surface quickly and inspiration flows freely.

> *"Kind words can be short and easy to speak,*
> *but their echoes are truly endless."*
>
> MOTHER TERESA

Courageously and continually affirm aloud, "I have good health," "I have love and harmony in my home" and "I have success in my future." Believe and do not doubt. For a few minutes each morning and again in the evening, repeat phrases tailored to your own special needs, such as:

✧ "God is guiding my steps."

✧ "New opportunities are strewn across my path."

✧ "Something great is going to happen today."

✧ "One door may have closed, but a window is opening."

✧ "Joy is overflowing from me onto others."

✧ "I give thanks to God for my ever-increasing good health."

Avoid "hard times" talk. Erase all thoughts of negativity and acknowledge the positive at every possible moment. I remember the lyrics from an old song by Don Moen that I heard many years ago: "And now let the weak say, 'I am strong.' / Let the poor say, 'I am rich.' / Because of what the Lord has done for us. / Give thanks." For when we ponder upon the good, and speak optimistically, expecting positive results, it can bring such thoughts and words into manifestation.

A minister once told a story about a woman who had a dream one evening that an angel escorted her to heaven. There, she was taken to an exquisite mansion. When the woman walked into the foyer, she noticed that the house was filled with doors. To the right and to the left, there were doors everywhere.

Curiously, the woman asked the angel, "What are all those doors?"

The angel replied, "Let's open them and find out."

First, they opened the door to their right, and inside there was "a great idea" that would have more than replaced the job the woman had, years before, lost. "But," the angel uttered to the woman, "You held on to negative thoughts, believing that nothing good would ever happen to you again."

Within the next door was "a wonderful new friendship." "However," the angel explained, "because someone betrayed you long ago, you became so bitter and discouraged that you stopped expecting great things for your future."

The following door contained "a golden opportunity." "Yet,"

the angel described, "Due to past setbacks, you said it was, 'too late' and you were 'not talented enough' to pursue and accomplish new dreams."

In her dream, the woman was shown that she'd been so full of doubts and fears that she'd missed out on forthcoming joys, blessings, and opportunities, which were symbolized by the doors.

What will you say? Don't hinder yourself from reaching your full potential by saying "no" or that "you can't." Surely, then you won't be able to achieve your goals. But, those people who say "yes," and "I can," do.

Never limit your vision for yourself or your future. Speak loving, positive, expectant, faith-filled words, and you will see a marvelous adjustment in your viewpoint. You can achieve what you say, so with your empowering words, strive to make your aspirations stunning realities.

Day seven:

God wants you to live by choice, not by chance.

"For as he thinks in his heart, so is he."

Proverbs 23:7, NKJV

You possess a great and wonderful power. It's a gift that was given to you at the moment of your birth by almighty God.

"So what is this power?" you may ask. God gave you free will . . . the power to *choose*.

> **An old fable once read, "What the sword
> shall give and the sword shall take is forged
> in the furnace in the choices you make."**

Many years ago, after a sudden and untimely death that had taken my mother, I lived alone in a small two-room apartment in one of the worst areas in the city. I had no resources or connections, and all the circumstances appeared to be stacked against me.

Some days, it didn't look like I would make it through the adversity, as I replayed over and over again in my mind the conditions surrounding her death. Alone in an unsafe part of the city, I easily could have chosen to take the wrong road and just given up on life. Destitute, frightened, and confused, and searching for answers, I found solace in my local library. Combing the shelves for Biblical and inspirational material, there I discovered a little book called *Your Greatest Power,* written in the fifties, by J. Martin Kohe. The title of the book caught my attention. So I sat down in a chair, in the corner of the library, and read the following:

> *Millions of people are complaining about their lot, disgusted with life . . . and the way things are going, not realizing that there is a power which they possess which will permit them to take a new lease on life. Once you recognize this power and begin to use it, you can change your entire life and make it the way you would like to have it . . . filled with joy.*

I realized that by the good choices I made now and in my future, I had the power to transform my adverse situation, instead of allowing adversities to negatively change me. For, I discovered, we always have a choice about which way we view our situations and what we are going to do about them. If our child spills a glass of milk, for example, we may not be able to change what has happened, because we see the spilled milk all over the table—that is a physical reality. However, we can change our attitude towards it, not letting ourselves get upset and angry, and this, ironically, alters reality.

Only you determine your worth, and ultimately your successes. For, it is your choices, not your circumstances, that will mold your future.

Each day, are you making conscious choices? Prior to doing something, do you really think about it? Or, are you living on autopilot? Before proceeding with a decision, do you stop and ask yourself, "How do I really feel about this choice?" and, "If I make this decision, how will it affect me in six months, or a year or two from now?"

Consider this very important question when making decisions: "Will what I am about to do take me closer to, or further, from my goal?" If the answer is "closer," then proceed. If the response is "further from," then reevaluate your choices.

Turning back to the Bible, a passage from Mark says, "And no one puts new wine into old wineskins; or else the new wine bursts the wineskins, the wine is spilled, and the wineskins are ruined. But new wine must be put into new wineskins" (Mark 2:22, NKJV). In the same way, beginning in your own thoughts, you can choose to let go of past hurts, setbacks, and disappointments to make room for the new, wonderful things that God wants to do in your life.

So, reach out to those aspirations which are before you and choose to set your thoughts on the good, on the just, and on the admirable, and do not consider any other avenues of thought. Think about it this way: Your mind is a revolving door. When a defeating, discouraging thought comes in, spin it out!

Choice is the key. You have options. There are good alternatives. You can begin anew. Maybe you can't control your circumstances at this moment, but you can control your choices. Edgar Allan Poe once wrote, "My personal library has two thousand books in it. Unfortunately, they are all copies of my first book." However, the lesson here is that, despite this, Poe did not choose to center his attention on the problem. In its place, he worked on a solution by using his creative energy to persist in writing. Centering his attention on new possibilities for the future, Poe went on to become an illustrious writer and poet, and his works continue to influence literature in America and around the world.

Take on a bold and courageous attitude by choosing to spend 95 percent of your time living your life with joy and purpose and 5 percent or less thinking about problems.

No matter what has happened in your life, *the power to choose* a better way to live is available to you now. For I know that you are equipped with inner strength and courage.

This past year, I have been corresponding with an incredibly brave gentleman from Ohio who has been fighting cancer. "The medical tests said I had 24 months to live," he recently wrote, "But six years later, I am alive and still choosing to believe that God has a healing in my life."

Month after month, in each correspondence, this devoted husband and father never complains. He doesn't dwell on doubt or bitterness, or let the unjust circumstances pollute his mind. Rather, he chooses to stay hopeful and positive. He smiles, regardless of pain. Many people wonder, "How does he have such endurable optimism?" Well, he told me, "It is a choice. . . . I refuse to yield to negative thoughts, because I know that we are all loved by a caring and loving Lord."

A day at a time, this gentleman chooses to look for opportunities around him to make a difference in the lives of others, as he continues his volunteer work at the children's hospital. His goal is to spread joy, to offer an encouraging word, and to lend a helping hand to children and their parents. "I have an insatiable quest that there are still some of God's special-needs children that I can help. And I find strength in focusing on them," he once wrote. And with a sense of selflessness, in another note he advised, "Catherine, the secret to true happiness honestly is found in what we can do for others." Yes, our choices can be very private, but as with this dear gentleman, countless men, women, and children can be positively influenced, and reap great benefits.

For the next 24 hours choose to put this Bible verse into practice and see how your day has been altered: "Whatever is true, whatever is honorable, whatever is just, whatever is pure, whatever is lovely, whatever is commendable, if there is any excellence, if there is anything worthy of praise, *think about these things*" (Philippians 4:8, ESV, italics mine).

When I lost my mother over 25 years ago, I never dreamed at that time that God would use that adversity as a way for me to help and encourage others through my columns, books, shows, products, and countless testimonies of God's love and faithfulness. Trust God, seek His will, and choose to courageously follow His nudges forward. And, "It is God who works in you . . . to fulfill His good purposes" (Philippians 2:13, NIV).

WINDOW FOUR

LET GOD'S WILL BECOME YOUR REALITY

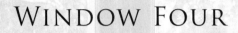

"Your talent is God's gift to you.
What you do with it is your gift back to God."

LEO BUSCAGLIA

DAY ONE:

YOU'LL KNOW YOUR CALLING BY HEART.

"Every good and perfect gift is from above, coming down from the Father of the heavenly lights, who does not change like shifting shadows."

JAMES 1:17, NIV

There comes a time in every life when a person might ask: "Where do my real talents lie?" or "Where do I belong?" And on occasion, he or she might look up at the vastness of the clear blue sky and wonder, "What does God want me to accomplish in my life? What's God's will for me?"

I believe that part of the answer to these questions lies in a narrative that I once heard about the early life of Mother Teresa. Late one afternoon, she was questioning her purpose and quietly asked a wise minister, "How do I truly know God's calling in my life?"

The minister responded quite profoundly, "You will know by your happiness. Profound joy of the heart is like a magnet that indicates the path of life . . ."

Thus, as you think about your future course, is there a profound joy in your heart because of whom you are with and what you are pursuing? What do you really like doing? Are you being gently nudged toward a particular path or in the direction of a specific need?

Five years from now, if there were no obstacles in your path, what dreams would you have implemented? If your potential were unlimited, what kind of life would you create for yourself and your family? It's never too late, so start now and follow your calling forward.

Last fall, I was traveling to New York City by train. I looked around the boarding dock, and there were so many different train tracks. One was going to the right, another to the left. Some tracks were facing due north and others were heading to the south. To the average person, it was confusing which track the train would take to reach its destination.

After I boarded the train, jokingly, I said to one of the conductors, "How do you know which track is which, as there are numerous tracks going in different directions?"

I'll never forget how the conductor replied. He said, "I know I am on the right track *by the way the train runs*." Likewise, when we are pursuing our destined purpose, we may have a sense and a knowing in our hearts and souls that this is where we belong. When we are in "the right place," "on the right path," and have found "where we belong," in our hearts, we will be happy and our daily work will be a pleasure.

When you discover your destiny, you'll find your joy.

There is a place for you. I know that God has entrusted you with extraordinary gifts and talents with which to enrich the world. You must keep striving, following your heart, and allowing your faith to press you ahead to find that open window. Challenges in your life may actually be opportunities that boost you to an exciting new place.

Therefore, take a step onward, just as the children of Israel walked forth on dry land, as God parted the Red Sea onto the path that He made for them. "And thou didst divide the sea before them, so that they went through the midst of the sea on the dry land" (Nehemiah 9:11).

But remember, the children of Israel had to get up and walk. You also have to get up and move forward. If Jesus can say to a raging sea, "Peace, be still" (Mark 4:39), and it obeys Him, He can certainly control and supply your needs. If He can utter, "Daughter, your faith has made you well" (Mark 5:34) and a woman is healed, He can definitely forgive your past mistakes and start you on a brand-new life.

You are destined to leave your signature on this generation, for you have everything within your reach to fulfill your great purpose. Keep in mind, it's not like being the right caller to win a radio station's contest; you are already a winner, because your calling is ordained by God.

✧ Stop thinking about the "should haves" and "what might have beens."

✧ Don't let people talk you out of your innermost dreams.

✧ Be open to how your dream unfolds; it might change course.

✧ Forge your own path. And with sincere earnestness, reach forth to what "can be" and "will be," remembering as you move forward that achievement in your personal or career life takes time.

Every person will face pressing problems at some point in their lives. Still, it's often not the problems, but how you deal with them that makes the difference. How do you play the cards that life deals you? Let the following fascinating story serve as an inspiration to you.

In the 1950s, a new highway was constructed along a Kentucky throughway, and with this interstate the majority of the customer traffic was diverted away from a town that housed a local restaurant. The owner of the restaurant watched with sadness in his eyes, as his successful business came to an abrupt end.

At 65 years old, the restaurant owner had experienced a number of personal and professional losses in his life. Nevertheless, rather than sitting back with his limited resources and feeling totally hopeless, possibly thinking, "My dreams are over," or "My best days have passed," the businessman decided he would make a fresh start. In spite of everything he had been through, he did not let bitterness taint his future. Instead, he followed God's will and persisted in doing what he loved to do, as God's destiny unfolded.

So, with a strong faith and his secret fried chicken recipe in hand, Colonel Harland Sanders began to market his delicious blend of 11 herbs and spices to restaurant owners across the country. Wearing his signature starched white shirt and white pants, Sanders was rejected and even made fun of on many occasions. Yet, he knew that we should not take another person's negative response or opinion as fact, or allow anyone to prevent us from becoming all that we can be. We must follow God's will and listen to our inner voice to guide us to what is best.

No one else can fulfill God's purpose for your life but you!

Understanding this principle, Colonel Sanders kept on going steadily forward with a fixed determination to make his dream a reality. He persevered, devoting himself to developing his chicken franchise business. And indeed he succeeded!

Today, Kentucky Fried Chicken has grown to become one of the largest fast-food empires in the world, employing thousands and thousands, with Sanders' organization donating large sums of money to worthy causes.

Remember, "A bend in the road is not the end of the road . . . unless you fail to make the turn." Like Colonel Sanders, no matter your age, losses, or limited resources, God can still use you and your gifts in a miraculous way.

I've heard it said that to attain success we must work, wait, and win. Most often, those who are at the top of the ladder were not just immediately placed there. With sweat on their brows, persistently, they climbed there, one steep step at a time. On their quest, they may have taken steps back or they might have even been intentionally pushed aside. But somehow, somewhere, they found the strength to get back up and climb on to achieve their heart's desire.

> *"It's a funny thing about life; if you refuse to accept anything but the best, you very often get it."*
>
> W. Somerset Maugham

We never ask for the challenges that life places before us. However, as we continue to move forward, we discover that these very obstacles form our strength, character, and resilience.

I like this beautiful poem by an unknown Confederate soldier.

I asked God for strength that I might achieve.
I was made weak that I might learn humbly to obey.

I asked God for health that I might do greater things.
I was given infirmity that I might do better things.

I asked for riches that I might be happy.
I was given poverty that I might be wise.

I asked for power that I might have the praise of men.
I was given weakness that I might feel the need of God.

I asked for all things that I might enjoy life.
I was given life that I might enjoy all things.

I got nothing that I asked for—But everything I had hoped for. . . .

Almost despite myself, my unspoken prayers were answered
I am among all men most richly blessed.

Therefore, let us enjoy each day of our journey . . . and take pleasure in the simple blessings of life. Let's discover our purpose, our area of calling—and really focus on it, knowing that whatever we pursue, we must do it with all our hearts. And like a magnet, profound joy will draw itself to us . . . and happiness will be ours.

DAY TWO:

AWAKEN AND TAP INTO YOUR VAST POTENTIAL.

"Beloved, I wish above all things that thou mayest prosper and be in health, even as thy soul prospereth."

3 JOHN 1:2

It was late in the afternoon and the day had been gloriously sunny. I had just spent an hour walking briskly up and down the beach. Listening to the surf and breathing in the sea air, I felt rejuvenated. The temperature hovered at around 80 degrees and, staring out into the vastness of the sea . . . I could *dream*.

I've always been a dreamer. Poet and biographer Carl Sandburg once wrote, "Nothing happens unless first a dream." For first we must dream, and after that . . . we can create the life of our dreams.

What's on your mind today? What are you allowing to motivate or drive your thought processes? When we think back on our childhoods, for many of us that was a time when it seemed as though, "All things were possible." Thereafter, we grow up, and perhaps go through challenges and disappointments, and then we convince ourselves that the dreams that we once had in our youth would now be impossible to implement. And so we let them go.

But you can still live out the purpose of the dreams of long ago. With God as your guide, nothing is beyond your grasp. Someone may have put their foot out and tripped you. Yet, I am asking you to get up and find the courage you need to pursue those dreams again. Arise, and swim upstream if you have to, in order to reach your full potential. Maybe you have always been last. But you have the favor of God in your life, and with that, you have the ability to dream and to make those dreams come true.

"If God is your partner, make your plans big!"

D. L. MOODY

Create a "dream board." Buy a white poster board and assemble pictures to represent the things that you desire to come into your life. Imagine what you would be doing in each area of your life—your health, your career, your personal life, and your leisure activities—if you were guaranteed success, because creating mental pictures builds inroads into your subconscious. Thereafter, find pictures that reflect the life you want to live. Cut out photos from magazines—pictures of places you'd like to visit, the home that you'd love to own, the career that you hope to achieve, the people you'd enjoy helping, the family you would like to have, the things you wish to do, the peace of mind you'd like to experience, and the goals that you want to accomplish. Glue the images onto the board and place it where you can view it daily. Add to your dream board often.

There is no "I" in team, so work with God "as a team" to find your life purpose. Regardless of past setbacks, adverse experiences, or current circumstances, all things are *still* possible.

I'd like you to keep true to yourself. And never give up on what you really desire to do. Start—just begin. Perhaps you can start by sharing with those you trust a goal from your dream board, so that you are held accountable to act on it. Your aspirations are not that far away, unless that is where you decide for them to be.

"But I didn't come from the right background," you might say. "I was told I'd never make anything of myself," or, "Achievements come to other people, not to me."

The other day, I was vacuuming in between the cushions of our sofa, and found some pennies and nickels. So, I turned the vacuum off and gathered the loose change.

How many of us see pennies in between our sofas, or a single penny on the street and think, "Oh, it's just a penny, it's insignificant." Then, we fail to pick up the pennies and put them to good use.

Maybe somebody caused you to feel worthless. Possibly you have had years of disappointments. Or else, in the darkness of the night, you have temporarily lost your way. Now, you feel like a penny that no one wants, that's hidden in between the cushions of a sofa or lying on the side of the road.

The good news is that God is interested in what others may deem insignificant. Every person has tremendous value. So ask God to restore your hopes and dreams. He can renew your life, because He wants to use you in a powerful way to make a difference in the lives of others.

On the surface, you could be the least likely to succeed and may not seem qualified. Outwardly, you might not be part of the in-crowd, or perhaps your material possessions are few. But, you were created by almighty God, and just as God gave Samson the strength to make the walls of a Philistine temple crumble to the ground (Judges 16:30), He has given you incredible inner strength and phenomenal gifts. So be strong and courageous. You have love, conviction, determination, wisdom, resilience, and fortitude within your heart, and those attributes will allow you to prevail over challenges, and they will carry you far in this life.

Samson's story provides powerful lessons. At his birth, which was miraculous because his mother had previously been unable to conceive, Samson's parents were told by God's messenger that their son was to deliver Israel from the Philistines, who were oppressively occupying the land. Samson was set apart for God's service and made a vow that he would never cut his hair, as a sign of obedience (Judges 13:5).

God gave Samson superhuman physical strength. However, rather than serving God as he had promised, Samson embarked on a life of lust, sin, and indulgence in worldly pleasures. Samson lacked self-control and was full of conceit.

Later, he fell in love with a woman named Delilah (16:4). The Philistines offered her money if she could tell them the secret of Samson's formidable strength. Delilah tricked Samson into revealing his secret, confiding in her that his strength was in his hair. So, while Samson was asleep, Delilah had her servant cut off his hair, and thereafter his vigor was gone.

The Philistines then captured Samson, blinded him, and put him in jail. Samson had little hope. But, day by day, he contemplated his mistakes, realizing that every compromise brought consequences. Samson repented, prayed, and yielded his life to God.

A celebration was being held by the Philistines, so they took blind Samson out of jail to ridicule him in front of the large crowds in the pagan temple of the Philistines. Each of Samson's hands was touching a pillar, and he prayed for God to strengthen him just one more time.

With all of his God-given power, Samson pushed the pillars apart. He collapsed the temple and thousands of the Philistines perished, disrupting their nation, so that Israel was able to come out from under its control. Because Samson was awakened, he was able to use his potential for good.

Describing God's power as a creator, the Prophet Amos said, "He who forms the mountains, creates the wind, and reveals His thoughts to man, He who turns dawn to darkness, and treads the high places of the earth—the Lord God Almighty is His name" (Amos 4:13, NIV). Amos reminds us that God can do anything. And this same God, who "shaped the earth from nothing," "formed the mountains," and "created the wind," can help you to take a seemingly hopeless situation and transform it into victory.

Tap into your potential and move forward more quickly by:

1. Changing self-defeating habits through shifting your focus from yourself onto others.
2. Breaking away from unconstructive influences.
3. Coming to terms with what happened yesterday and ceasing to dwell on it.

Remember, your past is no hindrance to God's saving grace, for "The Lord is near to all who call upon Him" (Psalm 145:18).

Try tapping into different channels that interest you and will help put you on your path to fulfilling your God-inspired dream. You will know very quickly if you've found the right direction—the window will either open or close. Either way, you will know where you stand. I'm fond of this quote from Albert Einstein: "When the solution is simple, God is answering."

Recently, a Michigan resident wrote to me and recounted how she had been through many storms in her life: sickness, divorce, a bout with depression, and several job losses. "But God was consistent in His guidance and always there to cover me and carry me through," her note stated.

In her letter, she described how she has always been determined to live a full and productive life. So she chose to go out on a limb, rekindle an old dream, and pursue an opportunity to go to nursing school. Although it was difficult, with a can-do attitude, she embraced her dream and pressed on toward the future. She wrote, "Today, I believe I am serving God's purpose in helping those in need."

Are you seeking direction? Try this approach: Take the focus off yourself and look for ways to be a blessing to someone else. There is no better way to receive help and direction in your own life than to focus on others.

At this moment, you are one choice away from a fresh beginning, another path, a different direction. Awaken and tap into your vast potential. Arise! The time is now, for I believe in you! Windows are about to swing open. And as sure as the sun rises each morning and sets in the evening, success will be up ahead for you.

It was getting late on that day of my stroll, and the beach was clearing out. I looked at my watch: it was 5:40 P.M. Look at your watch. What time is it? This is a destiny moment for you. It's time to reclaim your dreams and fulfill the vast potential of your life. Don't miss this opportunity . . . for God has a blessing for you.

DAY THREE:

ACCEPT THE GREAT LIFE THAT IS WAITING FOR YOU.

"For My thoughts are not your thoughts, neither are your ways My ways, saith the Lord. For as the heavens are higher than the earth, so are My ways higher than your ways, and My thoughts than your thoughts."

ISAIAH 55:8-9

How many insignificant things do you hold on to in your life? Do you carry with you feelings of inadequacy, fears, and worries?

Are you crippling yourself by refusing to forget a wrong? Or do you cling onto past rejections, resentments, and regrets? And, if you release them, what can God give you in their place?

I was told a story by an acquaintance of mine, about a little girl who loved fashion, and in particular, jewelry. One afternoon, she and her mother were at the shopping mall, and as they stood at the checkout line at a department store, the girl saw a pretty, plastic pearl necklace hanging on a display.

The girl approached her mother and asked, "Mommy, can I buy that pearl necklace?" And without skipping a beat, she implored, "Please?"

Seeing the expression of delight on her daughter's face, the mother said softly, "Okay, honey, I'll get the necklace for you. But you must take good care of it." And with that, the mother reached into her purse and paid two dollars for the toy necklace.

The girl's heart was soaring, when she opened the package and slipped the pearls over her head onto her neck. She just adored those pearls, took care of them, and wore them everywhere.

A few months passed and, one evening after dinner, the little girl's father sat down next to her on the couch. He began reading a storybook to her and nonchalantly asked, "Honey, will you give me your plastic pearl necklace?"

Stunned, the little girl blurted out, "Daddy, no! Not my pearls! I love them. I can't give them to you," she insisted.

"Oh, don't worry," he said, "Forget about it, honey, keep the pearls," and he resumed reading the book.

Another week went by, and the father asked his daughter again, "Are you ready to give me your pearls?"

The little girl fought hard to hold back tears and answered, "Oh, no, I can't give you my pearls!" She clung to them, saying, "I can't give them up."

Hugging her trembling shoulders, the father whispered, "Don't get upset, you can hold on to the necklace."

Several days later, when the father came home from work, the little girl was waiting for him at the door. She swallowed hard and managed to stretch out her arm, as she declared, "Here, Daddy," and she handed him her beloved pearl necklace.

The father knelt down and gave her a big hug and kissed her forehead. With one hand, her father held the plastic pearls. But immediately, with the other hand, he reached into his jacket pocket and pulled out a square, red velvet box. "This is for you," he uttered, with a huge grin on his face.

With love, the father looked at his daughter directly in the eyes, as the little girl slowly opened the box. And when she saw what was inside, tears of happiness ran down and streaked her radiant face. The girl was speechless. For within the velvet box was a new necklace . . . a strand of exquisite *genuine* pearls.

All along, the father had the new necklace waiting for her. However, he was hanging on to it until his daughter was ready to release the two-dollar strand of plastic pearls. It was only then that the father could give his precious daughter the real treasure.

> *"God has given you one face, and*
> *you make yourself another."*
>
> WILLIAM SHAKESPEARE

Could it be that, as in this story, God is waiting to advance us toward His will, granting us the desires of our hearts? But first, we must *let go* of the limitations, pain, and heartache of the past and accept the great life that is waiting for us.

Here's an exercise that you can do right now: Hold a small stone in your hand and imagine that that stone has, contained within it, something you need to release—a painful past incident, bitterness toward someone, or an unfair or worrisome circumstance. Next, acknowledge the hurt, and cast the stone away. And with it go all those negative feelings.

Remind yourself that letting go is a step-by-step process. Here are three effective ways to release pain and regrets, and thus, create space for a storehouse of new blessings:

1. Forgive those who hurt you, by praying The Lord's Prayer, daily. And allow God's forgiveness to flow from you, towards those who upset you. Luke 11:4 (NIV) says, "Forgive us our sins, for we also forgive everyone who sins against us."

2. Stop clinging to unjust circumstances, by refusing to rehash or continually talk about them. Soon, they will fade way significantly. 1 Corinthians 13: 4-5 (NIV) imparts, "Love . . . keeps no record of wrongs."

3. Use affirmations to combat negative feelings. A reader corresponded with me and said that for years she had blamed herself for all the things that went wrong in her family. Thus, to fight against her loathsome thoughts, she started keeping a journal. Twice a day, once in the morning and again in the evening, on each page she would write affirmations such as: "I am a generous, caring person," "I'm in control of my mind and my body," and "I am strong and will rise up from this condition, stronger." Habakkuk 2:2 tells us, "Write the vision, and make it plain upon tables, that he may run that readeth it."

Remember, you might have been "down" for a short while, but you're not "out." Hence, let go of what was, to make room for what *can be*.

"One doesn't discover new lands without consenting to lose sight, for a very long time, of the shore."

ANDRÉ GIDE

In the Scriptures, when Joseph spoke of his brothers selling him into slavery, he said, "As for you, ye meant evil against me; but God meant it for good" (Genesis 50:20, ASV).

Joseph's brothers were jealous of him because he was greatly favored by his father, so when Joseph was just a teenager, they cruelly threw him into a pit to die. Then they changed their plans and decided to sell him into slavery instead. Joseph was thereafter sent off to a foreign land as a slave. But God's plan for Joseph was far superior to his brothers' wicked actions. Joseph knew that God was in charge of his life and he accepted His will.

Years later, Pharaoh called on Joseph to interpret his dreams. Joseph did so successfully, and Pharaoh rewarded Joseph by promoting him to a position of great authority. When their land was beset by famine, Joseph's brothers traveled to Egypt to buy the grain the family needed. Joseph recognized them and let his brothers know who he was and that he was alive. Sorry for their betrayal, his brothers were forgiven by Joseph and reunited with him.

So, do not be shaken, but stand on His promises and lift your face toward Heaven and believe that God will make your crooked places straight. God's Word says, "I will bring the blind by a way they did not know; I will lead them in paths they have not known. I will make darkness light before them, And crooked places straight. These things I will do for them, And not forsake them" (Isaiah 42:16, NKJV).

As with Joseph, life has a bigger plan for you, too. There are happiness and success in your future. Therefore, keep your hopes high, and in the morning, wake up and say with confidence: "I can still accomplish my dreams," "I'm getting better and better," and "God has more ahead for me." He is always there; God is with you every step of the way, and He'll get you where you need to be.

He knows best. Forget what happened yesterday and look for the miracles before you.

At this moment, God has a present for you. Untie the wrappings; open the box, for inside it is the gift of a brand-new, precious day, filled with unsurpassed joys, love, and extraordinary wonders. Open your arms and embrace them. This is your time. You have earned it. Be happy and enjoy what is to come.

DAY FOUR:

LET DOWN YOUR NETS OF FAITH AND BE FILLED WITH AN OVERFLOW OF BLESSINGS.

"We live by faith, not by sight."
2 CORINTHIANS 5:7, NIV

Luke chapter 5 tells how the apostle Peter and his fellow fishermen were up all night in a boat trying to catch fish. However, in spite of their great efforts, their nets remained unfilled. These fishermen were professionals, so they knew that nighttime was the best time to fish, and they were in an area known for abundant catches. They did everything they could . . . yet still they came up empty. They had not caught so much as a single little fish. So, they went back to the shore, washed their nets, and wanted to forget about the whole failed experience.

Sometimes, do you just feel like quitting? Is it one setback after the other?

Are you waiting and waiting for something, with no response? Or have you ever tried and tried to accomplish something and then come up empty? Did you get discouraged and concede defeat?

The Bible account of the fishermen continues: that day Jesus was teaching by the lakeside, which was crowded with people. He saw two empty boats and got into one of them and asked Peter to push out a short distance from the shore. When Jesus finished speaking, He instructed Peter to "Put out into the deep water and let down your nets for a catch."

Peter was tired, frustrated, and filled with doubt, and replied, "Master, we worked hard all night, and caught nothing." Yet, realizing that God can work miracles for us, Peter decided to obey Jesus, anyway, declaring, "But at your bidding, I will let down the nets."

When the fishermen tried again, they succeeded! Their nets were so full of fish that they stretched to the point of breaking and even began to tear. The fishermen signaled to others for help, for even with two boats, because of the abundance of fish caught, they were so weighed down they had begun to sink.

Just when it appeared that all was lost, only a bit further out, there was victory. And the results were far better than the fishermen could have ever imagined.

There is nothing that you are coping with today that is too difficult for God to conquer. Have faith. He can change the most hopeless situations.

Don't miss this moment in time: This month, you can get that wonderful break you need. This week, a window may open to new opportunities. And today could be the day that you prevail over what looks impossible.

Look away from disappointments and, with a prayer of thankfulness, cast out your nets of faith, and utter:

✧ "No matter how large my obstacle, it can be overcome."

✧ "My goals may appear unfeasible, but they can be achieved."

✧ "Despite all the odds stacked up against me, I will succeed."

✧ "In spite of what the reports say, I still have a lot of loving and living to do, so I'll press on."

A setback will not pull you down. A rejection won't hinder you. A sickness is not going to stop you.

The other day, I received a letter from a New Jersey woman who wrote how, in 2006, she was diagnosed with end-stage liver disease and was told she would have liver cancer within the year. Terrified and losing strength daily, she went to her prayer room to talk to the Lord. She spoke to Him of what the reports had said, even though her faith told her she would be healed.

Daily, the woman submitted herself to God's will. She waited expectantly on Him, making the decision that she was not going to give into fears or be filled with doubts. But she was going to take hold of faith, "expecting a miracle," believing that, "her situation would circle around in her behalf," declaring, "'I'm coming up out of this better.'"

Through it all, she explained that she had grown in faith, peace, patience, and compassion, bringing her to a spiritual level beyond where she had been when everything was going right.

At the conclusion to her incredible letter, I blinked away tears as I read: "Catherine, it is 2010 and I have no scar tissue, all my blood tests are normal, and I have gained my muscle mass back. When I took my MRI test, it said the contour of the liver is now normal! The word *Believe* is displayed all over my house, inside and out. My body has been rebuilt, so I can have more time to tell the world about God's Son, my Lord and Savior, Jesus Christ."

Where is your faith today? And how can you increase it? Every day, you can start exercising your faith with this process:

- ✧ For easier reading and understanding, pick up an NIV (New International Version) or a Good News Bible.

- ✧ Look up in your Bible, or on the Internet, Scriptures dealing with your specific need, such as a need for healing, protection, peace, direction, or relationship or financial help.

- ✧ Next, speak these verses aloud.

- ✧ Afterwards, thank God for the miracle He has *already* provided. Talk as though your issue has successfully been resolved.

- ✧ And believe, confidently expecting that, if it is according to God's will, you'll receive the blessing.

"[God] is a rewarder of them that diligently seek Him."

HEBREWS 11:6

Faith is a key ingredient for receiving your miracle. Therefore, why don't you step out and try it? Stand strong and say, "Enough is enough," and have the courage to go forward in faith. If you start, if you just take that first step ahead, God will do the rest.

Day Five:

Strive for what's in your heart.

"O, my Father . . . thy will be done."

MATTHEW 26:42

In the early 1980s a nun from Alabama had an inspiration from God to build a television studio. She had no experience in construction, financial planning, or television operations. Guided by a firm faith, and placing her trust in the providence of God, she went outside on her property and put white rags around some trees, planning where the studio would be.

The property's maintenance man saw her mapping out the 50-by-150-square-foot area and asked, "What are you doing?"

Confidently, the woman stated, "We need a studio, and this is a reminder to the Lord to help us build it."

The maintenance man looked at her curiously, "Does the Lord need a reminder?"

Envisioning the studio, she smiled, "Certainly, it can't hurt to remind Him . . . "

With unyielding conviction, this woman's sights were set on this goal, and she had steadfast faith that the necessary means would be provided to achieve it.

Shortly thereafter, someone in town heard about the woman's dream to build a television studio, and he offered her 50,000 dollars to begin the project. And so it began.

That money was enough to clear the land and start the construction, but it soon ran out. Nothing further happened for a while. It would have been easy to give up, for every time this woman thought the road was clear, there were additional delays. Nevertheless, she did not waiver. She trusted God, prayed, believed, and with joyful expectation, anticipated the television studio in the making, which would be used for God's kingdom.

Subsequently, another person privately donated some funds for the project, and a little more construction was done. Step by step, very slowly, the television studio was being built.

Days and months went by, and more waiting, more hoping and praying. Then, all of a sudden, a couple donated a large sum of money to finish the building. And at the appointed hour, the 65,000-square-foot facility of The Eternal World Television Network was completed. That woman in Alabama was Mother Angelica, a cloistered Catholic nun, and she had acted on God's invitation to do the impossible. And through Him, a broadcast center was built that today has become the largest religious media network in the world. EWTN transmits programming 24 hours a day to more than 118 million homes in 127 countries worldwide.

Did you ever stop for a moment amid the busyness of life to seek God's will? Have you asked Him to guide you as you make decisions about your future? When was the last time you questioned Him, as in, "What would *you* want me to do, Lord?" Or else, have you prayed to God, as Jesus did, "Lord, not my will . . . but *Thy will* be done"?

Paul wrote, "Therefore, be ye not unwise, but understanding what the will of the Lord is" (Ephesians 5:17). How can you discover God's will? Well, here are four recommendations I've put together for you:

1. Read the Bible and get to know your Scriptures. For the mind of God is shown through His word.
2. Keep a strong connection with God. Through prayer, He can reveal His will into your heart.
3. Utilize your past experiences and assess your individual interests and abilities.
4. Consider the counsel of Godly people.

When God calls you, He will provide the way, as He did in the life of Esther in the Bible. God's hand called her to fulfill an important role. Esther was an Israelite and a woman of deep faith and was placed in the position of queen. When she heard that a law might be passed to make it legal to kill all Israelites, Esther trusted that God would bring His people through the difficulties they faced. Thus, she went boldly forward and asked the favor of the King to spare her life and the lives of her people. The King granted her request. And as a result of Esther's faithfulness, courage, and influence, she saved an entire nation.

God will "direct you in the way you should go" (Isaiah 48:17, NIRV), making "all things work together for good" (Romans 8:28, NLV), and making "the crooked roads . . . straight, and the rough ways smooth" (Luke 3:5, NIV). Every day, continue to ask Him to direct you, to fulfill His plan, and to show you the way.

A reader e-mailed me and explained how she had been involved in an abusive relationship. For years, fears had pushed her faith aside. Yet, she found the strength to end the relationship and began to seek God's will and purpose for her life. "Instead of creating my own alternative route, thinking that my ways were better than God's, I prayed and asked God to show me the best path that He had set for me," she noted. Her attitude was completely *Not my will, but Thy will be done.*

This reader described how, several months later, she seized an opportunity, changed career directions, and decided to go to night school. Coincidentally, in one of her classes, sitting next to her was a handsome young man. They started dating and two years later they got married. She concluded her note with, "Life is now better than I ever imagined."

> *"Trust the past to the mercy of God, the present to His love, and the future to His providence."*
>
> St. Augustine

Last night, I read a lovely letter from a Rhode Island gentleman who wrote, "For almost 50 years now, I have walked with the Lord. It's been great, a great life. Naturally, there have been mountaintops and valleys, but one thing I am sure of is that God has a calling on each of our lives. And God's plans for those who love Him are beyond what the eye has seen, ear has heard, or mind has conceived."

> *"Faith never knows where it is being led, but it knows and loves the One who is leading."*
>
> Oswald Chambers

God works in the lives of ordinary people like you and me. And He wants to do great things for us. Keep seeking His will; strive for what's in your heart, and the purpose for your life will be revealed.

Day six:

Quitting is not an option.

"And He did rescue us from mortal danger, and He will rescue us again. We have placed our confidence in Him, and He will continue to rescue us."

2 Corinthians 1:10, NLT

It's been a rough week. You're run down, disheartened, worried about the days ahead. Thinking that your dreams are deteriorating, facing another dead end, and feeling hopeless, the voices inside your head might be telling you, "Forget it," "You don't have a chance," or "Give up."

Maybe you have been left behind and are wondering if anyone can help you. And in a low moment you say to yourself, "I just don't care anymore." You're ready to shrink back and give up.

However, let me ask you a few questions: Are you going to permit a present challenge, a setback, or a rejection stop you from accomplishing God's will for your life? Are you going to give up now on God's dream, settling for the status quo? Of course you are not, because you have come too far, worked too hard, and sacrificed too much to stop now.

Take into consideration this approach: Think of each past

experience as a gust of wind that propels you higher toward your destined purpose. I want you to keep in mind that you have not exhausted all of your options. There is God-given strength within you. Be determined that you won't sell yourself short and quit. You have something special about you, with a destiny to fulfill. So, do not underestimate your worth or your great potential. Trust God—He has an amazing future set out before you. And soon you will come through your struggles more faithful, fervent, confident, and blessed.

There is a Tibetan proverb that says, "Even if you have failed at something nine times, you have still given it effort nine times." Moreover, what may, at first, appear to be "a failure" can actually prove to be a stepping-stone that creates for you a better, more harmonious, and more blessed life.

Early one morning, a friend of mine, Donna, was leaving for work. She lived in a condominium complex and every Tuesday, before she left her home for her office, she would take out her trash, throwing it in a large dumpster by the parking lot.

One Tuesday, Donna left for work earlier than usual. As she did every week, she brought out a bag of trash to toss into the dumpster. However, this particular morning, before she threw the trash bag in, she heard something. Stopped in her tracks for a moment, she listened to a faint scratching sound within the dumpster.

"I wonder what that noise is?" she mused, as she gingerly peered into the dumpster. Because it was rather dark outside and the dumpster was somewhat full, Donna couldn't see to the bottom.

Time seemed to stand still, as she wondered what to do next. Yet, something in her heart told her to "stay there and wait."

Instantaneously, Donna heard a slight meow. Barely audible, she gazed into the dumpster again, and this time she saw a tiny black-and-white kitten jumping up the side of the dumpster, trying to get out. Stunned, Donna watched the kitten's attempts to leap out, but each time the tiny animal slipped back down to the shadowy bottom. The kitten tried again and again, but nonetheless kept falling down.

With her heart beating fast, Donna reached in, scooped up, and rescued the frail little kitten from the dumpster. She then took the animal to a veterinarian and, with a little love and care, she helped it back to a clean bill of health.

Donna kept that sweet kitten and named him "Miracle," as he is a reminder that, regardless of your situation, if you do not give up, there is always hope. "God had me exactly where I needed to be, at the exact time I needed to be there," she exclaimed.

Just as God arranged for my friend Donna to be there for this kitten on that early morning, God is there for you. He hears your cries for help, and He hasn't forgotten you.

"The Lord will fight for you, and
you shall hold your peace."

Exodus 14:14, NKJV

The apostle Paul tells us in Ephesians 6:11-18 to put on "the full armor of God," so that we might stand firm in the battles of life. Every day, imagine putting on your armor for strength.

✧ The Belt of Truth surrounds all other pieces of armor and makes them impassable to worldly assault.

✧ The Breastplate of Righteousness symbolizes our heart being fortified against attacks made on us.

❖ The Shoes of Peace will carry us over obstacles and direct our path in His Eternal Peace.

❖ The Shield of Faith provides assurance of the faithfulness of God and His word.

❖ The Helmet of Salvation guards our head and mind from destructive thinking and temptation.

❖ The Sword of the Spirit represents the Word of God—His powerful secret weapon that protects against all evil.

Whatever challenges come your way, know that you are not alone. God's sovereignty reigns over all of your problems. Someday, you will look back on these days and wonder how you had the strength to endure. Then you will remember that your faith in God gave you the strength.

> *"There is only one way to bring peace to the heart, joy to the mind, and beauty to the life; it is to accept and do the will of God."*
>
> WILLIAM BARCLAY

A nurse, Kim, whom I am acquainted with, told me that in a hospital emergency, she sometimes writes the patient's vital signs in pen on her palm. "A piece of paper can be lost; a chart can be misplaced, so that way," Kim explains, "in an emergency situation, I don't forget very important information."

Likewise, God has "you engraved in the palm of His hand" (Isaiah 49:16). He has prepared a life overflowing with joy in which He wants to lead you. Difficult times are not going to last forever. I believe a season of blessings is approaching. And the same Hands that carry your name will reach down and lift you up, and you'll experience a miraculous, life-altering rescue!

DAY SEVEN:

THE BLESSING IS WITHIN YOUR REACH.

"Do not be conformed to this world, but be transformed by the renewal of your mind, that by testing you may discern what is the will of God, what is good and acceptable and perfect."

ROMANS 12:2, ESV

While traveling on a train from Manchester to London, a young British woman began thinking about the characters in an original novel that she hoped to write one day. Creative thoughts and unique ideas were filling her mind, but she didn't have paper or pen with her. So, for the four-hour train ride, all she could do was think and imagine the unlimited possibilities ahead.

From an early age, this young woman had dreamed of becoming a writer, and now her aspiration was beginning to take shape. But then tragedy struck. It was one adversity after another. She lost her beloved mother. Her marriage ended. And she found herself destitute, raising her daughter alone, surviving on financial assistance from the government, depressed, and feeling like a complete failure.

Yet, this budding author found the fortitude to persevere,

and was later quoted as saying, "Rock bottom became a solid foundation on which I rebuilt my life."

She drew on her adverse personal experiences, and on an old typewriter, she worked and reworked her writings. Diligently, she changed and edited her book's chapters many times over, ensuring that she was producing her best work.

In 1995, she completed the manuscript for her first book. And although her manuscript was rejected by twelve publishers, this determined young woman kept on trying. Finally, a publisher agreed to publish the book. In spite of that achievement, the editor told her to "get a day job," for she'd never make enough money to live on just writing children's books. She had no platform, resources, or connections.

However, negative predictions didn't stop this woman. She kept growing, learning, and persisting, and refused to allow limitations or past failures to take her off track.

Within five years, J. K. Rowling's Potter books became a publishing phenomenon. They have broken sales records, received prestigious literary awards, been made into top-grossing movies, and garnered worldwide attention, selling more than 400 million copies.

When we dream a really big dream, remember, God is not going to simply drop it in our laps. We must work hard for it. So, let's not just sit back and wait. You are capable of *more*. Prepare, stay alert. And set your dream in motion. Similar to the people of Israel in the Old Testament, you may have wandered off and experienced obstacles and stumbling blocks, but God has a Promised Land in your future. Regardless of limitations, past setbacks, or undeserved hurts, you can still realize your heart's desires and achieve your destined purpose. The blessing is within your reach, for God says,

✧ *"I am with you and will watch over you wherever you go, and I will bring you back to this land. I will not leave you until I have done what I have promised you"* (Genesis 28:15, NIV).

✧ *"Do what is right and good in the Lord's sight, so that it may go well with you and you may go in and take over the good land that the Lord promised on oath to your forefathers"* (Deuteronomy 6:18, NIV).

✧ *"The righteous keep moving forward and those with clean hands become stronger and stronger . . ."* (Job 17:9, NLT).

So, whatever you yearn to do, get underway, bit by bit, to make it come true. For example: If you love to perform onstage, join a local theater company and utilize your gifts. If you'd like to write a book, get a journal and begin writing one page a day. If you dream of purchasing your own home, start adding each week to a "new home fund."

> *"I find the great thing in this world is not so much where we stand, as in what direction we are moving."*
>
> OLIVER WENDELL HOLMES

I just read an article about a 99-year-old gentleman who continued to develop his potential, in spite of difficult circumstances. And at 99 years old, he just graduated from college. Do you think your best days have passed you by? Well, you're never too young or too old to dream, and to bring about what you set out to complete.

> *I like what Thomas Edison said when he was asked, "Are you successful?" His answer: "I start where other men leave off."*

When you are trying to accomplish a goal, evaluate what you are trying to achieve by checking:

1. Your motivation.
2. Your attitude.
3. Your objective.

If you have thoroughly checked these three things out prayerfully, and found each to be in the will of God, you cannot fail.

In my first book, *A New You,* I told a cute story that I had once heard about a little fish swimming in the vast blue ocean.

The tiny fish was listless and weak, as he huddled near the big coral reef. Then, a large, mighty fish swam past him, concerned. "What is the matter, little fish?" he asked. "Is there anything I can do to help you?"

The little fish wearily replied, "I am so tired and thirsty."

"Well," stated the big fish, "Start by taking a nice, long drink of cool water and surely you will feel better and get your strength back."

The little fish quickly answered, "Oh no . . . I can't! I just can't!"

"But why?" questioned the big fish.

"I do not want to drink too much water," said the little fish, "because I am afraid it will all run out!"

"Run out!" exclaimed the big fish. "Run out! That's a good

one. This is the Atlantic Ocean. Run out! Ha ha ha," laughed the big fish, as he swam away.

This story illustrates that we live way below our privileges. God has given us abundant blessings within our reach and, as His children, we are heirs to all of these.

Walk away from the ordinary, and step into the extraordinary. Do not dwell on the stumbling blocks that could be before you. You can prevail over the obstacles that are placed in your way. How? By staying extremely focused on your goals. God sees your capabilities—He knows where you've been, and what you can become. Keep believing and reaching beyond where you are now, and don't be afraid to aspire to the highest and best.

Yes, you may be "a little fish" in "a big ocean." And perhaps the odds against success are staggering, and the dream, outwardly impossible. But, somehow, someway, it can happen, because God specializes in using unlikely people, in out-of-the-ordinary ways, to accomplish His great purpose.

> *"Expect great things from God;*
> *attempt great things for God."*
>
> WILLIAM CAREY

At all times, keep hope and courage alive. God has new possibilities with which He wants to entrust you, so keep watch. There are always signs if you are open to them. The blessing is within your grasp. So, go ahead and reach for it.

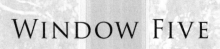

WINDOW FIVE

RALLY YOUR SUPPORTERS AND LOOK FOR HELP

"Don't walk in front of me, I may not follow.
Don't walk behind me, I may not lead.
Walk beside me and be my friend."

ALBERT CAMUS

DAY ONE:

"SAVING GRACE" WILL COME FROM ABOVE.

*"Two are better than one; because they have a good reward for
their labour. For if they fall, the one will lift up his fellow:
but woe to him that is alone when he falleth; for he hath not
another to help him up."*

ECCLESIASTES 4:9-10

On a television news station, I saw a dramatic dog rescue a few
years ago. A German shepherd was stranded in the raging, rising
waters of the Los Angeles River. Moment by moment, hour by hour,
the distressed dog struggled to try to get to safety. But there was no
way out. The dog was trapped for a prolonged period of time.

When I watched the video footage of the frightened animal
scrambling trying to find its way onto dry land, the extenuating
circumstances looked hopeless. And I asked myself: *Where can
help come from?* Well, in a short time, my question was answered,
as *help came from above.*

I could hear the sound of a helicopter's engine going into the
isolated area, as it flew forward and then backward. An incredibly
brave fireman, on a harness, hanging from that helicopter, was
hoisted down, close to the river, near the animal.

The fireman reached out his arms and tried to grab hold of the frightened dog, with no success. Yet, he didn't stop trying. However, when he did get close to the dog, the terrified animal bit the fireman's fingers. Undaunted, he attempted the rescue again. And suddenly, he was able to seize the dog! As he strongly held the large animal in his arms, they were both hoisted back up into the lateral helicopter. The dog was miraculously saved.

This phenomenal rescue reminded me: When it appears that there is no way out of your situation, your help, too, *will come from above.* In the Old Testament (NLT), Isaiah 63:9 says, ". . . In His love and mercy He redeemed them. He lifted them up and carried them through all the years." Outside forces might be pulling you down. But don't fear. As the fireman lifted up and rescued the dog, God will lift you up and carry you through the difficulties.

Do you feel that there is no way out of your present situation? Are you worried about your future because you are ensnared in an unforeseen circumstance? Or maybe you are trapped in a legal issue. But no matter how small or large your needs may be, God is there for you. With Him, you can start over, you can recover, and you can change directions, for it is never too late to achieve your heart's highest goal. Beyond this difficult time, a new, glorious day is at hand.

Take a moment and do a self-check. Do you trust God? Do you believe that when you experience difficulties, help will come from above? Are you on the lookout for God to intervene and provide a solution to your problems?

Consider this approach: As you go through your day, keep four little words in the forefront of your mind: "Be on the lookout." God works in mysterious ways. His specialty is doing the impossible. And help can come from unexpected places.

Tip: Having a Godly mentor can accelerate your success.

✧ Does all appear to be lost? Be on the lookout for a person to intercede. Out of the blue, you may bump into someone, and that encounter can change the course of your future.

✧ Is your circumstance at a standstill? Be on the lookout, while keeping hope alive. All of a sudden, you may be at the right place at the right time and everything will fall into place perfectly.

✧ Have you suffered a defeat? Be on the lookout for a new idea, as you continue to persevere. Unexpectedly, you could be offered an amazing opportunity that brings new dreams to fruition.

✧ Are you going through a tough time right now? Be on the lookout, as you reach out and ask for help. God knows how to arrange the situations and people that you need to get your life back on track.

I love the parable that Jesus told about the Good Samaritan. There was a man lying hurt and wounded on the roadside. A passerby walked on the opposite side of the road and looked across toward the helpless man, but he did not cross over to the other side to assist him.

Another person came hurrying along, anxious to get out of the desolate area before nightfall. He passed by when he reached the wounded man, and turned away without offering any aid.

Then, along that lonely road came a man riding on his donkey. He stopped immediately, and ran to the man's side. "This man needs my help," the Samaritan thought, as he bandaged the stranger's wounds and lifted him onto the back of his donkey. The Good Samaritan walked beside the poor man, holding him on his donkey until they reached an inn, where he cared for him all night. In the morning, when the Samaritan had to leave, he gave the landlord money and asked him to take care of the injured man. "Look after him," he said, "and when I return, I will reimburse you for any extra expense you may have" (Luke 10: 35, NIV).

The Gospel writers remind us that Samaritans were not liked and were, in fact, viewed as inferior; they were considered and treated as outcasts of the day. Yet, the Good Samaritan unconditionally took the time to take care of the wounded man. And his benevolent actions and compassion are an example of God's unconditional love toward us.

"I am the bread of life. He who comes to Me shall never hunger, and he who believes in Me shall never thirst."

JOHN 6:35, NKJV

One of the most incredible letters I ever received was from a naval submarine officer who was stationed on a submarine deep in the Adriatic Sea. The officer wrote via e-mail, "In the mess deck, I found your article lying on a table. I have no idea how it got into the ship and it helped me so much." The officer told in his e-mail that he had been praying and, a few moments later, the article had miraculously appeared to him at the just right time. And my encouraging words gave him hope, comfort, and renewed strength to not give up. "Regardless of what is going on in the world, your article reminded me that God is with us," he continued.

"The Lord is the strength of my life; of whom shall I be afraid? When the wicked came against me to eat up my flesh, my enemies and foes, they stumbled and fell. Though an army may encamp against me, my heart shall not fear."

PSALM 27:1-3, NKJV

Accordingly, with expectation, "be on the lookout," and trust God. Just as the fireman and the German shepherd were hoisted up into the waiting helicopter, God will take you up higher and higher with His saving grace from above. He will restore your peace and joy, and lead you ahead into a life of blessings.

"Trust God as if it all depends upon Him and work as if it all depends upon you."

ROBERT JONES

DAY TWO:

YOU BENEFIT YOURSELF WHEN YOU LOVE AND LEND A HAND TO OTHERS.

"Give and it will be given to you. Good measure, pressed down, shaken together, running over, will be put into your lap. For with the measure you use it will be measured back to you."
LUKE 6:38, ESV

An old Chinese proverb says,

> *If you want happiness for an hour, take a nap.*
> *If you want happiness for a day, go fishing.*
> *If you want happiness for a week, get promoted.*
> *If you want happiness for a year, inherit a fortune.*
> *If you want happiness for a lifetime, help others.*

Being connected to people, through service, is one of life's greatest joys. And moreover, offering a helping hand to others can bless us in ways that we never thought possible, bringing us greater joy and fulfillment.

On the road of life, we can encounter challenges all along the way. But I believe if we persevere through life's shadows by doing kind deeds, soon light will shine forth into those darkened places, and we will be lifted up from despair into the glow of the sun. A wise, longtime friend of mine, Ann Marie said, "I think if you stop thinking about your own situation, and focus on others—along with prayers and faith in God—you can get through anything."

So, instead of sitting around day after day, worrying and wondering how to solve our own problems, we must take the focus off of ourselves by doing something nice for someone else. Let's keep busy making a positive difference in the lives of our fellow human beings.

Here are a number of ways to extend your hand and heart: Coach a sports team. Help a neighbor with yard work. Take someone who doesn't drive to run errands. Tutor a child. Or mentor a young person. Your joy will be full as your love flows out and brightens the lives of others.

Foster friendships by opening your door to others. Invite friends, neighbors, or associates into your home for more relaxed conversations.

I receive letters from people who have lost their jobs and they explain that one way they get through changes and transitions is by volunteering. It may be at animal shelters, soup kitchens, or hospitals. They also lend a hand at their children's schools and assist the less fortunate. A dear friend, Vivian, takes her petite white dog to visit the residents in senior citizen facilities. And I heard about a family who bakes dozens of cookies periodically for their local fire and police departments. They even send homemade baked goods overseas to our servicemen and women, as a thank you for the selfless work that they do.

Surprise someone with a small gift. Mail an encouraging greeting card to a person who may need cheering up. Uphold another in prayer. And lend a listening ear. Often, a person who is sad or frustrated just needs someone who will listen. This will go a long way when someone has lost a loved one or suffered a similar loss.

Compile a list of at least a dozen out-of-the-ordinary ways that you can be a blessing to others. Post the list on your refrigerator. Each day, perform at least one good deed.

Every new day is a gift from God. That's why we should make a decision to be generous with our affection, love, and praise. Last week, I saw a sign in a store window that read, "Only love matters." So let us be grateful for those nearest and dearest to us, and let's express over and over again how much we love, admire, and appreciate them.

God repeats the word *love* hundreds of times in His Scripture. Here are a few examples that stand out:

"Love one another, as I have loved you" (JOHN 13:34).

"Love your neighbor as yourself" (JAMES 2:8, ESV).

"Be likeminded, have the same love, being of one accord, of one mind" (PHILIPPIANS 2:2).

The Open Window

"If you love me, keep my commandments"

(JOHN 14:15, NKJV).

Therefore, we must have love because "love never fails"
(1 CORINTHIANS 13:8, NIV).

Sometimes, *how* you say something counts more than *what* you say. Tenderly and sincerely utter, "I love you" to your spouse, and "I'm thankful for you," and "You mean the world to me." Convey to your loved ones, frequently, the qualities that you admire the most about them.

Hug your children daily and watch their eyes light up with joy as you tell them, "You are God's gift to me," "You amaze me," "You're a miracle," and "I love you so much." Help build up a young person's self-esteem by genuinely praising their one-of-a-kind abilities, efforts, and good works. Encourage their dreams, regardless of how big or small they may be, by declaring, "I believe in you," "Always try and be your best," and "You have the ability to accomplish your goals."

You can also assist in boosting the spirits of your family members, friends, and co-workers, by sincerely complimenting them. Regard all people as important. Use their names when speaking to them. And don't gossip, be critical, or talk badly about others. I like the wisdom that my friend's father always imparts: "Once the toothpaste is out of the tube, you can't get it back in." Thus, try not to say negative words about anyone. Instead, help improve the lives of others by being kind, friendly, and gracious to them. Let's make up our mind to be positive, for if we live, think, and act positively, we will attract positive results.

"How far that little candle throws its beams!
So shines a good deed in a weary world."

WILLIAM SHAKESPEARE

Today, I know the world needs your light to shine brightly to make it a better place. Humbly ask God to provide you with a way for His light to shine through you. And, one step at a time, by acts of helpfulness, kindness, and as you give to others, you will have a lifetime of happiness!

Day three:

Humor enriches your life and lessens burdens.

"You will have sorrow, but your sorrow will turn into joy."
JOHN 16:20, NLV

You can banish tension, worry, and concern with laughter. If you smile, your burdens will be lightened. You probably don't think of laughter as medicine, but it is believed to help people live longer.

There is a direct correlation between humor and good health. There is more and more evidence indicating that our thoughts, feelings, and attitudes not only play an obvious role in our mental health, but are also contributors to our physical well-being. Laughter can make us feel good and can go a long way in helping us to cope with challenging times. It's a powerful remedy for stress and may help to protect us against negative emotions by defusing worries or anger, simultaneously relaxing the whole body. Studies show that a good belly laugh can do wonders for breathing, blood pressure, our immune system, muscle tension, digestion, and more.

Our daughter Gabriella is always twirling through the house. Every time someone sees her, she is giggling and spinning. So one day, I asked her, "Honey, why are you always spinning around?" She replied, "I am so happy, I twirl!"

Maybe you won't be spinning through the house, but laughter has been called "inner jogging" because when we are engaged in a hearty laugh, every system in our body gets a workout. Laughing does not require any special equipment or clothing, and it doesn't cost anything. It's readily accessible and free of charge, just waiting to burst out and brighten our day.

Turn to the Book of Psalms, sing praises to God, and gain a greater appreciation for the importance of laughter.

✧ Psalm 126:2 (ESV) says, "Then our mouth was filled with laughter, and our tongue with shouts of joy; then they said among the nations, 'The Lord has done great things for them.'"

✧ Psalm 32:11 (ESV) says, "Be glad in the Lord, and rejoice, O righteous, and shout for joy, all you upright in heart!"

✧ Psalm 16:11 (ESV) says, "You make known to me the path of life; in your presence there is fullness of joy; at your right hand are pleasures forevermore."

"Well," you might say, "I have too many problems to have a sense of humor." Yet, did you know that humor is an incredible tool to use when you may feel like crying? Humor is one of God's marvelous gifts. It reveals the roses and helps to hide the thorns. It softens the harshness of life for you and others. Humor makes our heavy burdens lighter, soothes the rough spots in our paths, and eases the tension from our heavy workloads.

✧ Laugh at stumbling blocks and persevere, and then they can become stepping-stones to your goals.

✧ Use humor to smooth over disappointments, and soon they can turn into new opportunities.

174

✧ When you feel powerless against the events that sometimes occur, you can summon your sense of humor and gain strength.

A Connecticut reader sent me an exquisite hand-drawn picture of a puppy and wrote, "I am 60 years old and unemployed, but I continue to hope, and drawing gives me such joy." This reader delights herself in God and the talents He has given to her.

> *"Weeping may endure for a night, but*
> *joy cometh in the morning."*
> PSALM 30:5

Humor helps to keep things in perspective. It can draw our attention away from our difficulties. A lady from Missouri wrote to me and shared in her letter that having a positive attitude and good humor helped her as she healed from an operation. She described how she wrote down in a journal a list of all the happy things in her life, and rereading the list helped her to focus on her many blessings, and thus, improved her entire outlook.

We can improve our mood, too, and maintain a healthy balance by creating a "Humor First Aid Kit" to view whenever we need a good laugh. We can fill our kit with humorous mementos, books, CDs and podcasts, comics and cartoons. A friend of mine, Melissa, suggested, "Choose a computer screensaver at home or work that makes you laugh." Help others bring laughter and smiles into their lives by donating comic books or funny videos to your local hospital or library. Or gather your family and watch a funny television program or movie together.

Hang up pictures of your family and pets that make you chuckle.

Rally a few of your friends together and laugh with them. Laughter can ignite creativity and connect you to other people, so make humor a habit:

1. Clip a cartoon from the newspaper and send it to a friend.
2. Laughter can spark creativity, so inject good humor into your business environment in memos or meetings.
3. Set a time each day to focus on fun. Invite others to join in and bring humor into conversations by asking, "What funny thing happened to you today?"

One afternoon, I was leaving the grocery store and an elderly man was walking behind me carrying a large pink bouquet. I turned around and said to him, "Oh, you shouldn't have. . . . Thank you for these flowers, I love pink!" We both laughed and his step had more of a spring to it as he walked away.

A long-distance friend once told me that when she was in elementary school, her mother wrote in her autograph book a verse she would always recall. It read, "The world is like a mirror, reflecting what you do, and if you face it smiling, it smiles right back at you."

Smile for, like laughter, it is contagious. Be near people that are fun and optimistic, for it's great to be around people who laugh, announcing pleasure and humor to others. Encourage a child's infectious laughter. Play with your sweet pet for a mood boost.

Summon wit from your spouse, and ask older people to reminisce about happy memories. Humor strengthens relationships.

For the next eight hours, choose to smile more often. Smile at your family. Smile when you look in the mirror. Smile and nod a "hello" to everyone you see as you run your errands. Smile at your pets. Smile at others at your workplace and at your children's school. Then, notice how your outlook has changed. Is there anything different about you?

Here's a piece of interesting research: Daily, children and toddlers laugh on average 300 times, as compared to 15 times for adults. So, let's take a lesson from children!

Whatever makes you laugh, put more of it into your life. Laughter is the music of the soul. Utilize this priceless gift of laughter and add precious moments to your day. And soon you will be able to sing, as the Psalmist did, "You have turned my mourning into joyful dancing . . . and clothed me with joy" (Psalm 30:11, NLT).

DAY FOUR:

HELP IS AVAILABLE TO YOU RIGHT NOW.

"I lift up my eyes to the mountains—where does my help
come from? My help comes from the Lord, the Maker
of heaven and earth."
PSALM 121:1-2, NIV

The Book of Job in the Bible recounts the story of how Job, a blameless and upright man, suffered terribly, losing his family, his health, and his worldly goods. He despaired; he was angry at God and accused Him of denying him justice. Finally he challenged God in a duel of words . . . and lost. Job 38:1-2 (NIV) states, "Then the Lord answered Job out of the storm. He said, 'Who is this that darkens my counsel with words without knowledge?'"

Through his scores of trials, Job learned valuable lessons and trusted in the will of God. In the end, God restored to Job twice as much as he had lost and brought him blessings in the latter part of his life to compensate for the trials in his earlier years.

But as Job was experiencing these trials, friends rallied to support him. Scripture says, "Now when Job's three friends heard of all this evil that had come upon him, they came each from his

178

own place, Eliphaz the Temanite, Bildad the Shuhite, and Zophar the Naamathite. They made an appointment together to come show him sympathy and comfort him" (Job 2:11, ESV).

Are you scared? Does the future seem uncertain? Is your heart heavy and burdened with anxiety and unease? Are the tears falling fast? And do you often wonder, "Why?" and question, "Why did this happen?" or "Why am I going through this situation?" Well, you may not always know *why* you go through trials, but you can rally others for moral support, help, and assurance.

A correspondence from an Arizona reader advises, "Having a trusted friend and a network of support can be a shield to bear the bumps, hold the reins, show the right way to follow, and also be a companion through bad times. They can comfort on difficult days, and show us that rainbows do follow the clouds."

The Book of Proverbs is full of passages encouraging us to seek wise counsel:

✧ Proverbs 19:20: "Listen to advice and accept instruction, and in the end you will be wise" (NIV).

✧ Proverbs 27:17: "Iron sharpens iron, and one man sharpens another" (ESV).

✧ Proverbs 11:14: "Where there is no guidance, a people falls, but in an abundance of counselors, there is safety" (ESV).

Here are eight tools for how you reach out to others to help you through difficult periods in your life:

1. Talk to your best friend, a family member, a teacher, or mentor, and lean on them in times of despair.
2. Call your pastor, rabbi, or a member of your clergy. Share your feelings and perhaps they can offer gentle reassurance.
3. Get advice from someone who has expertise in the area in which you need help.
4. Ask your human resources office at your place of employment what counseling programs are available.
5. Call a 24-hour counseling hotline anytime if you need to talk to someone, especially if you are quite depressed.
6. Join a weekly support or special interest group. Look in the newspaper or online in the "events" section for community organizations that offer help or companionship.
7. Connect with a church-affiliated group; most churches and other religious organizations have all kinds of groups to help their communities.
8. Contact your town hall. Most towns and cities have Family Services departments that provide individuals with assistance.

I know a dear father who was brokenhearted because his son had made some poor choices, getting involved with substance abuse. And his son paid the consequences of this destructive decision for many years. The fight was long and difficult, yet with faith in God, his family's support, and the help of community groups, the battle was won. The son went into rehab and recovery houses, thus receiving the additional assistance he needed. And today, this young man continues to attend meetings and counsels others who are healing, helping them to reclaim their lives. "All the praise goes to God for my son's new choices," exclaimed the father. "I'm so proud of how he is overcoming barriers, and helping others, too!"

Setbacks are surmountable; problems will pass. They will be resolved. So don't accept your present condition as permanent. It's only temporary. In the meantime, get ahold of all the resources you require to get you through the tough times.

In the morning, at lunchtime, in the evening, or while waiting in a doctor's or dentist's office, I'd like you to read something inspirational to make you feel better.

✧ When in drugstores and grocery stores, look for magazines with articles that apply to your situation and read them.

✧ Go to the library and check out books and magazines on self-help.

✧ If something happens over which you have no control, say, "God, this is too much for me to handle, so I'm putting it in your hands." Then stop worrying about it and let God attend to it.

One of the most extraordinary letters I have received was from a man in a correctional facility. He wrote to say he and his co-inmates hold a prayer group in the evening and start the session with the reading of my weekly column. Thereafter, each person discusses what the column has meant to him or her, or what it has brought to him or her. Excerpts from his letter include, "We would like to thank you from the bottom of our hearts for providing us a little ray of sunshine and hope into the lives of people who are trying to regain or renew their faith and put their lives back together and become productive members of society again."

At this point, if you do not have the support system that you need, please allow me to offer my encouragement:

You can get beyond this challenge.
Cast off old hurts to make room for God's blessings.
Reach ahead. You have a purpose to fulfill.
You were born to make a difference in this world.
God loves you very much.

I once heard a poem by James Russell Lowell
I liked that I'm passing on to you:

. . . behind the dim unknown,
Standeth God within the shadow,
keeping watch above His own.

God wants to help you and be your true friend. And right now, listen as He is saying, "Do not fear, for I am with you, do not be dismayed, for I am your God: I will strengthen you, I will help you, I will uphold you with My righteous right hand" (Isaiah 41:10, ESV).

DAY FIVE:

LIFE EXPERIENCES, GOOD AND BAD, MOLD CHARACTER.

"Therefore, as God's chosen people, holy and dearly loved, clothe yourselves with compassion, kindness, humility, gentleness and patience."

COLOSSIANS 3:12, NIV

There was a chill in the air as a friend of mine and I walked into a neighborhood café for coffee. She was depressed and had called me and asked if we could meet and discuss her problems. "God has something wonderful planned for you . . . I know it," I said to her, when we first saw each other.

My friend looked at me, her eyes sullen, searching for hope, looking for reassurance.

Then, I encouraged, "He is just waiting for the right time."

It had been eight long years since my friend had left her thriving corporate career to start her own business. Although she is faithful, hardworking, creative, giving, and talented, for some reason, nothing had worked out for her. It was maddening. For just when it seemed as if a breakthrough would come, it turned into another dead end. Yet, through the ups, and mostly downs, my friend had gained tremendous know-how and experience.

"God is leading you as He always has. Have faith," I softly whispered, as we sat down at a round wooden table by the window. And I added, "He will lead you to the right position."

"You cannot glorify God better than by a calm and joyous life. Let the world know that you serve a good Master."

C. H. SPURGEON

Between sips of warm coffee, I told my friend, in my own words, a story that a reader had recently sent to me. In the story, a mother and her grown daughter were having a conversation in the kitchen while they were making a cake. The weary and disheartened daughter stood by her mother and explained how everything in her life had gone wrong. Her career was at a standstill, and she had encountered setbacks, been met with losses, made mistakes, and regretted some decisions she had made in her past.

The mother listened closely and then asked her daughter if she would like a taste of the cake she was mixing together in the bowl. The daughter replied, "Sure, Mom, I'd love some."

So the mother reached for her measuring spoon, poured some oil into it, and handed her daughter the tablespoon of oil. The daughter looked puzzled.

After that, the mother asked, "How would you like two raw eggs?"

Perplexed, the daughter answered, "No, thank you!"

Next, the mother offered, "How about some dry cake mix?"

"Yuck!" the daughter exclaimed, and questioned, "Mom, what are you doing?"

The wise mother replied, "All of these ingredients seem awful by themselves. But when you put them all together, they make a wonderful cake!"

As I finished this story, the smile across my friend's face told me that she understood what I was trying to say to her through this simple analogy. For no experience in your life, good or bad, has ever been wasted. It is your experiences, put together, that help mold you into the person you are destined to become.

My friend was encouraged when we left the café late that afternoon, and as I hugged her good-bye, I affirmed, "There is something great ahead for you. You will understand when it all falls into place."

A few months passed, and my friend called me with good news. Literally, in a flash, an opportunity with a local company had become available. And because she had tremendous credentials and experience, she was offered, and joyfully accepted, the job of her dreams!

Engage in face-to-face conversation. With the increased use of technology, it's important to still connect with one another via real person-to-person conversation.

- ❖ *Share a meal or meet a friend for coffee and talk.*
- ❖ *Arrange a daily or weekly walk with a neighbor to interact while exercising.*
- ❖ *Set up a weekly tennis or golf game with a business associate.*
- ❖ *Meet another mom in town and window-shop.*

Right now, you may be undergoing many challenges and there may be no solutions in sight. "When is my situation going to change?" you wonder, as you take a deep breath. "Why is God holding back and not answering my cries for help?" But do not let your "current circumstance" or this "season" of hardship to cause you to lose your faith and your confidence in yourself and recede

> *God is never early, He is never late, but He is always on time.*

from life and the opportunities that await you.

Just as the wind moves in a continuous motion and the tide changes directions, your situation, too, will shift its course. Maybe you have lost something, a job or a relationship, but you've also created space for something new to come along. As opposed to yearning for what used to be, try this: enjoy what you have *now* and *look forward to* what is to come. Now, begin to share what you've experienced with others, and perhaps form a support group.

✧ Meet for a monthly breakfast meeting with colleagues from your office and brainstorm new ideas.

✧ Start a moms' group where you can talk about raising children.

✧ Try forming an art, sewing, or knitting club so you can interact with others while being creative.

✧ Get involved in your community by establishing a center to help the less fortunate.

✧ Host a Bible study one evening a week and discuss spiritual lessons. Here is a great message from Matthew 5:1-12 (NIV) to get your group started. It's from the Sermon on the Mount, which is perhaps one of the most famous sermons ever preached. This section of it, called the Beatitudes, is Jesus describing the attitudes we should foster in ourselves and practice:

When Jesus saw the crowds, he went up on a mountainside and sat down. His disciples came to him, and he began to teach them. He said:

> *"To get the full value of a joy, you must have somebody to divide it with."*
> MARK TWAIN

Blessed are the poor in spirit, for theirs is the kingdom of heaven.

Blessed are those who mourn, for they will be comforted.

Blessed are the meek, for they will inherit the earth.

Blessed are those who hunger and thirst for righteousness, for they will be filled.

Blessed are the merciful, for they will be shown mercy.

Blessed are the pure in heart, for they will see God.

Blessed are the peacemakers, for they will be called children of God.

Blessed are those who are persecuted because of righteousness, for theirs is the kingdom of heaven.

Blessed are you when people insult you, persecute you and falsely say all kinds of evil against you because of me. Rejoice and be glad, for great is your reward in heaven, for in the same way they persecuted the prophets who were before you.

To be "blessed" is to be favored by God. And the Beatitudes are intended to give us a clear understanding of the blessings to be bestowed upon us, if we foster positive character attributes in ourselves, love others, and strive for righteousness in all that we do, despite the seemingly bad things that end up being rewarded or used for good.

Awhile ago, I heard about a philanthropist named Larry Stewart. For almost 30 years, this successful businessman anonymously gave over a million dollars to needy people. Often, he would roam the city streets, typically handing out 100-dollar bills to those in need. And he even recruited others to help him carry out his mission of love.

"Why did Larry Stewart perform these random acts of kindness to total strangers?" one might ask. Because he knew the pain of growing up poor and living in extreme poverty. Raised by his grandparents in a small town, there was seldom enough money for food or proper clothing. However, Stewart's earlier struggles were worthwhile, for he chose to use them in a positive and productive way. For, years later, his heart of understanding motivated him to serve others.

Hence, pay attention to your life's experiences. What has inspired you to be better? Stronger? More helpful to others? God cares about your heart and your character. So, earnestly seek Him; spend extra time in prayer. "Draw near to God and He will draw near to you" (James 4:8). He will come close, lift you up, and your experiences will get richer and fuller with each successive treasured day.

DAY SIX:

A GREAT ATTITUDE HELPS PAVE THE WAY FOR GREAT RESULTS.

"Be careful how you think; for your life is shaped by your thoughts."

PROVERBS 4:23, GNT

A wise dad wanted to teach his children a valuable life lesson, so one morning he planned to take the two lads on a long hike around the lake near their home. Before they left the house, though, he instructed the boys to bring their backpacks with them.

"I am conducting an experiment, boys," said the dad. "So don't ask any questions until we get home and I will explain then," he tenderly advised them. The boys agreed.

As they walked along the country road, from time to time the dad would bend down, pick up a rock, and place it in one of his sons' backpacks. Alternating between the boys, the dad would sporadically place rocks in their bags. Sometimes, however, he would stop for a moment, and take a rock or two *out* from one of their backpacks. This same scenario continued throughout the course of the day.

Late in the afternoon, the boys and their father returned home. When they reached the house, the two boys were tired.

Their backpacks were heavy with a variety of rocks, and they were thankful that they didn't have to carry them on their backs anymore.

Now warm and comfortable, sitting on their family room couch, one boy asked, "Dad, can you tell us now about your experiment?" The boys were curious, probing, "Why did you keep putting rocks in our backpacks and then taking some out?"

The father explained that, when he was a young lad, his dad had conducted this experiment with him, and that he had always remembered its important lesson.

"Today," the father described, "I gave you both an attitude test."

Stunned, the boys questioned, "What? What's an attitude test?"

"Boys," the father stated, "As we were hiking, I was listening carefully to everything you said, and whenever one of you complained or spoke negatively about a person or a situation, I picked up a rock and put it in your backpack."

The boys stared at each other, with wide-eyed, confused looks on their faces.

The father continued, "But, when either of you displayed a grateful, generous attitude—when you spoke of the best in others, and a belief in yourself, I removed a rock from the bag."

There were 60 seconds of complete silence, as the father asked his sons to take a look at the backpacks they had been carrying all day and said, "Wrong thinking, regrets, frustrations, and un-forgiveness are like those rocks—you can hold them in your mind, just like you carried them in your backpack. And if your mind becomes too cluttered with discouragement, it can prevent great things from happening in your future."

The father hugged his boys and concluded, "Always remember the power of a positive attitude. Pay attention to your thoughts. Listen to the words you use, and notice how you say them." Similar to this little story, we must choose wisely and not permit destructive, toxic thoughts to rule our minds.

What are you thinking this very minute? When you wake up in the morning, what dominant thoughts occupy your mind? For as the days and months past swiftly by, I realize more and more that our outlook, our attitude, what we think and the words we speak—they all influence everything around us.

If you're wrestling with a negative matter, I want you to ask yourself: Is this issue really worth my energy? Will this problem matter in a year? Here's an idea to help to bring you peace regardless of the difficulty: Call your clergy and have your house blessed. When the minister arrives, you and your family could gather in the living room to begin the blessing, which you might call "Celebration for a Home." The minister may hand you a prayer sheet, so you can follow along. Next, you might move from room to room. In the foyer, Holy Water might be sprinkled and you could pray, "The Lord shall watch over our going out and coming in." And in the office, "Teach us, O Lord, where wisdom is found, and show us the place of understanding." In the kitchen, "We shall eat in plenty and be satisfied." But before the ritual takes place, forget past setbacks, forgive everyone who has hurt you, and release all bitterness. And after the home blessing, you may find that you experience a newfound joy and peace.

Experience tells me that our attitude toward life and how we should conduct ourselves should always be like the Lord's. In Galatians 5:22-23, the Apostle Paul defined nine virtues, otherwise known as the Fruit of the Spirit: *"But the fruit of the Spirit is love, joy, peace, forbearance, kindness, goodness, faithfulness, gentleness and self-control"* (NIV). Here follow Scriptural passages touching on each of these nine virtues, which together encompass the Fruit.

Love: *"Love is patient, love is kind. It does not envy, it does not boast, it is not proud. It does not dishonor others, it is not self-seeking, it is not easily angered, it keeps no record of wrongs. Love does not delight in evil but rejoices with the truth. It always protects, always trusts, always hopes, always perseveres"* (1 Corinthians 13:4-7).

Joy: *"A happy heart makes the face cheerful . . ."* (Proverbs 15:13).

Peace: *"Blessed are the peacemakers, for they will be called children of God"* (Matthew 5:9).

Forbearance: *"Be joyful in hope, patient in affliction, and faithful in prayer"* (Romans 12:12).

Kindness: *"Be kind and compassionate to one another, forgiving each other, just as in Christ God forgave you"* (Ephesians 4:32).

Goodness: *"Love each other deeply, because love covers over a multitude of sins. Offer hospitality to one another without grumbling"* (1 Peter 4:8-9).

Faithfulness: *"Now faith is confidence in what we hope for and assurance about what we do not see"* (Hebrews 11:1).

Gentleness: *"And the Lord's servant must not be quarrelsome* *but must be kind to everyone, able to teach, not resentful"* (2 Timothy 2:24).

Self-control: *"Reject every kind of evil"* (1 Thessalonians 5:22, NIV).

The Bible also tells us to "Set [our] minds on the things that are above" Colossians 3:2 (ESV). So let me ask, what inspires you to have a good attitude?

1. The average person can spend 100 hours a year commuting to work. Utilize those hours listening to motivational CDs, programs, and podcasts.
2. Most people devote over an hour a day to doing household chores. Try making a CD or playlist of uplifting songs and listening to them while you do your chores.
3. While you're watching your favorite television show, use the 60 minutes to exercise. Walk on a treadmill, pedal a stationary bike, or do some strength training with free weights.
4. When you are on vacation, read a spiritual book and thereby develop a reservoir of newfound strength.
5. Use your refrigerator as a message board: every day, put a new message on it to inspire yourself and your family, who will see it whenever they get hungry!

Put memorable articles, family pictures, Bible verses, prayers, or motivational quotes on your bedside table, desk, or kitchen counter to fill you with joy.

Recently, our middle daughter, Gabriella, told us that she could not see the blackboard clearly at school. So I made an appointment for her to get her eyes checked. And, sure enough, the optometrist reported that Gabriella was nearsighted and needed glasses for distance. So we chose some pretty pink-and-white wired frames.

A few days later, Gabriella's new glasses were ready, and after school, we drove to the doctor's office to pick them up. I'll never forget the words my daughter spoke when she first put her glasses on. She couldn't contain her joy and enthusiasm as she looked around and exclaimed, "It's a whole new world!" Certainly, with clear vision, it was as if Gabriella saw the world for the very first time. Let us choose to see the world as she did, with positive expectation, vision, and enthusiasm.

I'm fond of this quote that a reader from Louisiana sent to me:

"Whenever you look back at your life, be positive.
Whenever you look at the present, be realistic.
Whenever you look to the future, be bold."
AUTHOR UNKNOWN

Your mind is a precious gift from God. So, as you go about your day, remember the Fruit of the Spirit: *love, joy, peace, forbearance, kindness, goodness, faithfulness, gentleness, and self-control.* And with a virtuous, bright disposition, you can positively shape your future and live a joyful, glorious life.

DAY SEVEN:

DEPARTED LOVED ONES ARE NEVER FAR AWAY.

"Blessed are they that mourn: for they shall be comforted."

MATTHEW 5:4

Looking down from the heavens, departed loved ones are always with us. The memories of their words, the warmth of their smiles, and the love of their lives are alive in our hearts, providing comfort. They are just a thought away and their wisdom can continue to give us strength for the challenges that lie ahead.

It was one of the last things a dear mother wrote in her journal before she died. "When God calls, I will let you know when I arrive on the other side. I will ask Him to send a storm on the day of the funeral."

Bright blue and sunshine filled the sky, as family members and friends gathered to fondly remember this mother. Not a cloud was to be found. The weather report called for clear and dry conditions for the next three days.

That afternoon, a luncheon was held in her memory and by 5:00 P.M. most of the guests had gone home. As the family was clearing the dishes from the dining room table, a loud rumble startled them. All at once, black clouds blanketed the sky and thousands of huge raindrops poured down in masses. Thunder and lightning filled them with solace, awe, and joy, as they found hope in the storm.

It's been said that death is far from being the end; rather, it's an open window to an existence larger, brighter, and more blessed than this one. "I lost my wife after 40 years of marriage," wrote a reader from Massachusetts. "We have four children and seven grandchildren, a blessing beyond words. A quote I read some months after my wife's death was, 'Death ends a life, not a relationship.' In my case, nothing has ever been so true."

Here's a comforting exercise that you can do right now: If someone you love has passed away—a parent, grandparent, spouse, or close friend—visualize that person by your side daily, watching over you, encouraging you to live to your full potential.

Even though our loved ones can look over the banisters of heaven, they can never feel sorrow over our trials, for they know, like the Lord does, that all things work together for good for those who love God and are called according to His purpose. His ultimate design for us is to have His love and live with Him eternally. Upon leaving this world, there is a realm of endless sunshine, for we are children of the light. Many people who have experienced the light of great love at the end of a tunnel before being brought back to earth have written about it in books. We have been given these various examples so that we know they are not coincidences.

Look at what the Bible says about eternal life:

John 14:1-4 (ESV) tells us, *"Let not your hearts be troubled. Believe in God; believe also in me. In my Father's house are many rooms. If it were not so, would I have told you that I go to prepare a place for you? And if I go and prepare a place for you, I will come again and will take you to myself, that where I am you may be also. And you know the way to where I am going."*

Romans 14:8 (ESV) states, *"For if we live, we live to the Lord, and if we die, we die to the Lord. So then, whether we live or whether we die, we are the Lord's."*

Revelation 21:1-4 (ESV) describes, *"Then I saw a new heaven and a new earth, for the first heaven and the first earth had passed away, and the sea was no more. And I saw the holy city, new Jerusalem, coming down out of heaven from God, prepared as a bride adorned for her husband. And I heard a loud voice from the throne saying, "Behold, the dwelling place of God is with man. He will dwell with them, and they will be his people, and God himself will be with them as their God. He will wipe away every tear from their eyes, and death shall be no more, neither shall there be mourning, nor crying, nor pain anymore, for the former things have passed away."*

Have you suffered a loss? Did you lose someone you love all too soon? Are you experiencing deep emotional grief? Begin your journey to healing by communicating your feelings.

✧ Lean on people who care about you and accept their help and advice.

✧ Embrace comfort from your faith. Pray. Light a candle. Attend a faith-based, spirit-filled church and talk to a member of your clergy.

✧ Converse with someone you trust or find a grief support group or a professional grief counselor.

✧ Join a bereavement support group in your area and share your feelings with others who may have experienced a loss.

Other means of healing through grieving can include:

✧ Crafting a collage: Try putting together, perhaps in a book, a collage of pictures of the person that has passed away. This will give you a chance to connect with special memories and times you spent together.

✧ Distracting yourself: Focus on something else besides your pain; go to a movie, the theater, a concert, or try a new hobby or creative outlet such as painting.

✧ Combating stress by taking care of your health: Get enough rest, eat nutritious foods, and partake in regular exercise.

✧ Reading books or listening to audiobooks by authors who have gone through similar situations and heeding their insights.

At the age of four, Colton slipped from consciousness during emergency surgery for a burst appendix, but then emerged from his life-threatening ordeal with astounding details about his time in heaven. His book, *Heaven Is for Real,* details meeting his relatives, including his sister, whom his parents had never mentioned to him, as she had died two years before his birth in a miscarriage. Vividly, Colton describes the beautiful colors of heaven, the many people there, the animals, and the angels who were singing to him to ease his anxiety, and how he even sat on the lap of Jesus. Colton's story brings me peace and comfort, as does this poem:

A POEM FOR THE GRIEVING

Do not stand at my grave and weep.
I am not there, I do not sleep.
I am a thousand winds that blow,
I am the diamond glints on snow.
I am the sunlight on ripened grain,
I am the gentle autumn's rain.
When you awaken in the morning's hush,
I am the swift uplifting rush
of quiet birds in circled flight.
I am the stars that shine at night.
Do not stand at my grave and cry,
I am not there, I did not die . . .
—*Anonymous*

In John 10:27-29, Jesus said, "My sheep hear my voice, and I know them, and they follow me. I give them eternal life, and they will never perish, and no one will snatch them out of my hand. My Father, who has given them to me, is greater than all, and no one is able to snatch them out of the Father's hand."

So, dear readers, I want to pass along to you the reassurance I feel when I look up to the stars at night and think, "My mother, great in her faith and thankfulness for the joys of life, must surely be in their midst." Sometimes, when the clouds part, I think of the light of her radiant smile and I know she still watches over me.

Window Six

Never Give Up

"When things go wrong, as they sometimes will,
When the road you're trudging seems all uphill,
When the funds are low and the debts are high,
And you want to smile but you have to sigh,
When care is pressing you down a bit,
Rest if you must, but don't you quit.

Success is failure turned inside out,
The silver tint on the clouds of doubt,
And you can never tell how close you are,
It may be near when it seems afar.
So, stick to the fight when you're hardest hit,
It's when things go wrong that you mustn't quit."

Author Unknown

DAY ONE:

WINDOWS OF OPPORTUNITY USUALLY SWING OPEN ON THE HINGES OF ADVERSITY.

"Count it all joy, my brothers, when you meet trials of various kinds, for you know that the testing of your faith produces steadfastness. And let steadfastness have its full effect, that you may be perfect and complete, lacking in nothing."

JAMES 1: 2-4, ESV

As I write, spring has come to the northeast, and with the weather mild and sunny, my husband and I recently decided to take our children to visit the zoo. We, along with scores of other people with big smiles on their faces, went through the entrance gate and canvassed exhibit after exhibit, peering in awe at the amazing creatures.

Enjoying nature's splendor, we walked up a short, tree-lined path, and stopped to marvel at the natural beauty of the towering 17-foot giraffes and their offspring basking in the zoo's open woodland. One little giraffe calf was sitting on the ground next to her mother, but in an instant, she got up and was on her feet. Then, the calf seemed to wobble and fall down. Yet effortlessly, she stood back up again.

My oldest daughter's hair fluttered about her face in the breeze and her blue-green eyes were wide open with curiosity, as she said to me, "Mom, with their long legs, I am surprised how quickly the calves are able to stand up."

I agreed. And at that moment, I recalled a book that I had read years ago about calves that had taught me a valuable life lesson. "Well, honey," I answered my daughter, as we stood still, arm in arm, "The calves have to get up quickly if they tumble, because if they're in the wild, they can fall prey to other animals."

Continuing, I told Lauren that when a mother giraffe gives birth, she does so standing, and the calf then drops to the ground from about six feet up, and typically head first. Quickly, I assured her, "The fall does not hurt the calf. However, almost immediately after birth, the mother teaches the calf, by actually *knocking the baby down*, to stand up on its own legs. The mother giraffe knocks the calf down *repeatedly*, for she wants to strengthen her little one in an effort to try to keep him or her safe for the challenges ahead."

"Mom, the calf learns to 'get up' by being 'knocked down?'" Lauren asked.

"Precisely," I uttered. And, as if reading my mind, I knew she sensed what I was saying.

When we arrived home, I went into the office to skim my shelf for the book *A View from the Zoo*, by Gary Richman. I found the copy and sat down on my wingback chair and began to read once more how the author described the birth of a baby giraffe:

> *The mother giraffe lowers her head long enough to take a quick look. Then she positions herself directly over her calf. She waits for about a minute, and then she does the most unreasonable thing. She swings her long, pendulous leg outward and kicks her baby, so that it is sent sprawling head over heels.*
>
> *When it doesn't get up, the violent process is repeated over and over again. The struggle to rise is momentous.*

As the baby calf grows tired, the mother kicks it again to stimulate its efforts. Finally, the calf stands for the first time on its wobbly legs. Then the mother giraffe does something remarkable. She kicks it off its feet again. Why? She wants it to remember how it got up . . .

I've thought about the birth of the giraffe many times. I can see its parallel in my own life. There have been many times when it seemed that I had just stood up after a trial, only to be knocked down by the next. It was God helping me to remember how it was that I got up, urging me always to walk with Him, in His shadow, under His care.

Have you been knocked down time and again? Maybe you've experienced an emotional "kick," or have suffered through various trials. But what can help is to keep in mind that the events in your life, even the most difficult ones, have meaning and value. And, just as they are for baby calves, challenges, obstacles, and "kicks" are a call to strengthen you, not to defeat you.

I love the story in the Bible that Jesus told about the widow who continued to persevere, even in the face of rejection. Beginning in Luke chapter 18, verse 1, the passage tells of a widow who had been wronged and wanted justice. The judge, who regarded neither God nor man, finally gave in because the woman was relentless in her cause. He said, "I will give her what she wants lest with her continually coming she wearies me."

God gave us that example because He loves it when we keep pressing on, persisting when we are tempted to quit, trying again and again and again if we don't get as far as we want. "God blesses the people who patiently endure testing and temptation. Afterward they will receive the crown of life that God has promised to those who love Him" (James 1:12, NLT).

*"Permanence, perseverance, and persistence
in spite of all obstacles, discouragements, and
impossibilities: It is this, that in all things
distinguishes the strong soul from the weak."*

THOMAS CARLYLE

To keep yourself strong and enhance your own level of perseverance while passing through difficult times, try this approach:

✧ Be optimistic. Optimism allows you to continue to persevere without being discouraged.

✧ Be resourceful. Keep trying all avenues to your goals, until you find a way to succeed.

✧ Be confident and don't worry about the little things. When dealing with small annoyances, gently redirect your focus back to your goal.

✧ Be a reasonable risk taker. For without a little risk, there is no reward.

✧ Be self-disciplined. View failures as learning experiences and keep moving forward through apparent setbacks.

✧ Be self-reliant, not letting anyone destroy your dreams. Follow your own path, and don't be too concerned about what other people think or say if you know you are following God's will for your dreams, rather than just your own without consulting Him.

God created you with a vast inner determination and resilience. Despite how many setbacks you have had, I'd like you to press on, daring to reach for your heart's desires. Stop looking at where you've been and begin to focus on where you can be today and tomorrow! Expand your range of possibilities. Go further. Don't wait. And if you stumble along the way or if someone trips you, get back up and start to move forward again.

If you knock on a door and nothing happens, you must knock again, and again and again. Solomon says in Proverbs 24:16 (NIV), "Though a righteous man falls seven times, he rises again." Therefore, if you fall down, get back up and try once more. The realization of worthwhile goals comes to those who persevere.

God is with you, so rest in His care, timing, and sovereign purpose. It is just a matter of time before you accomplish your dreams. So boldly look with hope and confidence to the future. Victories are forthcoming, with more joys, more blessings, and more rewards in store for you.

I still wonder sometimes why the knocks and kicks in my own life are so many. But then I receive letters from readers who say, "I feel like you are writing these words for me," "I want you to know how you have changed my life," and "Thank you for being there."

And instantly, with startling clarity . . . I know.

Remember what Edison said after he made thousands of efforts to produce illumination with the electric light: "I haven't failed. I've just found 10,000 ways that won't work."

DAY TWO:

DREAMS COME TRUE WHEN YOU WORK FOR THEM.

"I can do all things through Him who strengthens me."

PHILIPPIANS 4:13, ESV

There is an endearing story about a teacher who was instructing her students about the importance of persistence and determination. One morning, she stood in front of her blackboard and asked, "Class, who remembers the Wright Brothers?"

Quickly, a boy raised his hand and blurted out, "I do! They invented the airplane."

"That's right," uttered the teacher.

Then, she inquired, "Now, boys and girls, who knows Benjamin Franklin?"

Once again, almost every hand was raised and the teacher pointed to a girl in the front row for the answer. "Oh, he invented electricity!" the girl answered with enthusiasm.

Next, the teacher probed, "Who can tell me about Eli Whitney?"

More hands were raised, and a student replied, "He discovered the cotton gin that allows us to process cotton to make yarn."

Smiling, the teacher said, "Very good," and praised the children for their knowledge.

Yet, she asked another question, "Boys and girl, can you tell me who was Robert Jones?"

The students looked at each other, confused, their minds racing for the answer. Shuffling in their seats, finally, one boy shrugged his shoulders and admitted, "I don't know who he was."

The teacher declared, "No one knows who Mr. Jones was, because Mr. Jones gave up too soon."

That little analogy helped the children to realize that they should follow their hearts, believe in themselves, set goals, and, with unwavering determination, never give up.

"Real leaders are ordinary people with extraordinary determination."

AUTHOR UNKNOWN

Are you looking for an easy path to your goals, instead of the path you really need to take to accomplish them? Are you failing yourself by giving up too soon, even though you believe you can achieve something better than you have now?

"But," you may utter, "I have had too many challenges and setbacks to succeed." Well, I say, "We all have! But that doesn't mean you are finished. You are only finished if you quit!"

Here are three reasons you should not give up:

1. You can make a difference in the lives of others.
2. You deserve to be happy and to reach your full potential.
3. You may be a heartbeat away from success.

With a determined spirit, difficulties can't hold you back, delays won't stop you, and obstacles cannot get in the way. So, continue on with your dream, with steadfast determination and keeping God first place in your life, and there will be greater opportunities in the future for you to release your full potential.

Recall the captivating Biblical narrative about David and Goliath. Everyone was afraid of Goliath, because he seemed unconquerable and invincible. However, while other people ran away from Goliath in fear, young David didn't concede. Instead, David took the needed action, in faith, regardless of discouraging conditions.

So David and Goliath confronted each other—the huge Goliath with his armor and shield and a small shepherd boy, David, with only a slingshot and a pouch of stones. But, David kept his focus on God. He was confident and believed God would give him the strength to defeat the giant.

David then drew near to Goliath and said to him, "You come to me with a sword and with a spear and with a javelin, but I come to you in the name of the Lord of hosts, the God of the armies of Israel, whom you have defied . . . This day the Lord will deliver you into my hand . . . that all the earth may know that there is a God in Israel . . . the Lord saves not with sword or spear. For the battle is the Lord's, and He will give you into our hand" (1 Samuel 17:45-47, ESV).

Goliath then moved in to destroy David, but David quickly ran out to meet him. Then, David reached into his bag and slung one of his stones at Goliath's head. That small stone found its way through a hole in Goliath's armor, hitting his forehead, and the giant fell to the ground.

Most of us retreat and run away from our challenges. Alternatively, let's step out and go toward our challenges, as David did, and our giants—or, in our case, our stumbling blocks—will fall.

Recollect your victories. I'd like you to list on a sheet of paper a few incidences in your recent history when you tried for a goal and succeeded. This little experiment can give you a fresh outlook and help you to continue to work hard during tough times.

Earlier in the year, I received an inspiring letter from a 29-year-old gentleman from New York. His story was so remarkable, it left a lasting impression on me and I wanted to share it with you.

This gentleman explained that he's a sales associate at a gas and food store and recently was married to his high school sweetheart. "I am starting to build my dream as we speak," he wrote.

He conveyed how he grew up in a broken home, had no father figure, and was raised by a woman who took custody of him when he was a boy. For years, he found himself in standstill mode, yet, he always had a passion for hair cutting and styling. Even though he had been working since he was 16, he had no resources or means to follow his dream. Sensing God was calling him to new horizons, he was determined not to quit. So he found a cosmetology program, and after much research and some testing, he was qualified to begin the course.

Shortly after starting the cosmetology program, though, he hit another roadblock. Because he was a slow learner, he struggled and had difficulties with the curriculum. He thought his dream of becoming a hair stylist was over; however, God had another plan, and what seemed to be a closed door was actually a golden window of opportunity. The instructors placed him in special classes, which made him eligible for funds, allowing him to go to cosmetology school free of charge!

In his letter he revealed how, when he heard the incredible news, with tear-filled eyes, he bowed his head and prayed, "Dear God, I know I am weak right now, but this is my chance and I am going to take it. Please be with me. I know it is going to be hard and tiring, but I promise I am going to go all the way!"

The gentleman focused on his goal, working at his day job from 6 A.M. until 2 P.M. and going to cosmetology school at night. With the support of his wife and some precious relatives who believed in him, his hard work and determination paid off. Graduation day was one of the best times of his life! Thereafter, he recalled how so-called friends told him, "You are crazy," and "You will never get anywhere." Thankfully, he didn't listen to their negativity and, instead, determinedly pursued his passion. As time went on, the gentleman continued working at his day job and with his cosmetology license, he was able to cut and style hair at a local salon in the evenings and on weekends.

"I'm a great believer in luck, and I find the harder I work the more I have of it."

THOMAS JEFFERSON.

Toward the end of his letter he wrote, "Catherine, I am here to tell you that I am opening my own salon! An opportunity came my way, and I took it! What a road it has been. But your dreams are only dreams if you don't do the work and make them come true."

After that, he suggested four rules to live by:

1. Love God.
2. Love yourself and who you are.

3. Love others.
4. Go for your dreams.

Similar to this determined gentleman, God has called you to persevere. He will give you the strength to work hard and will bless your efforts.

"The difference between 'try' and
'triumph' is just a little umph."

MARVIN PHILLIPS

And soon, sometime, in some way, or through someone, in a likely unexpected and certainly extraordinary way, a glorious window will open for you!

Day three:

Tune out the naysayers, for great things wait beyond the barriers.

"For a great and effective door has opened to me,
and there are many adversaries."
1 Corinthians 16:9, NKJV

Are you overly sensitive to what people say? Have you been laughed at or have others made fun of you?

A reader from South Carolina wrote, letting me know that for the past eight years he has been working hard toward earning a degree in the medical field. He explained, "This goal was difficult to achieve because of the responsibilities of having a full-time job, a home, and a family to care for and support. Many people told me this day would never happen, that I should give up, but my struggles and hard work have paid off. I recently took the final exam, and passed."

So stay positively focused, and reject all distractions. Yes, people will be quick to tell you why you can't succeed, that you don't have what it takes, or that you'll never do be able to do "that." Tune out the critic. Turn a deaf ear to the naysayer. Be courteous toward others, certainly, but do not let those who purposely push you down rob you of your dreams.

Let's take a lesson from the weather; it pays no attention to criticism.

Beginning in Mark 5:22-43 (NIV), the Bible tells how Jairus, a synagogue ruler, pleaded with Jesus to come and heal his sick daughter. But, before Jesus reached Jairus's home, some people who had been at the house saw Jairus and told him that his daughter had already died. Jesus overheard the conversation. Scripture says that Jesus "ignored what they said," and then He told the synagogue ruler, "Don't be afraid; just believe."

They arrived at Jairus's house, and Jesus saw the confusion and heard all the loud crying. He went in and said to them, "Why all this commotion and wailing? Why are you crying? The child is not dead but asleep."

But they laughed at him. So after he put them all out, he took the child's father and mother and disciples, and went into the room where the child was lying. Jesus took her by the hand and said to her, "Talitha koum!" which means, "Little girl, I say to you get up!" And she got up at once and started walking around.

If adversaries or opposition come against you, do what Jesus did in this narrative: "ignore them, don't be afraid, just believe," and stay on course toward your goal. You must never let other people prevent you from becoming all that you can be.

Remember the Biblical wisdom from Amos 3:3 (NIV): "Do two walk together unless they have agreed to do so?" Today, ask yourself, "Do those who surround me 'add to' or 'detract from' my willingness to do what's necessary to achieve my goals?"

From this day forward, become aware of how you feel with certain individuals.

1. Steer clear of relationships with people who don't respect themselves. Why? They will be incapable of valuing you.
2. Pick your company prudently, and separate from individuals whose purpose is not to help, but to hurt.
3. Develop some new friends who support your goals and will celebrate your achievements.
4. Keep a positive and clean home environment.
5. Forget keeping up with the Joneses. Do not worry about what other people think, what they have, or what they are doing. Live the life *you* want to live.
6. Eliminate counterproductive habits, such as repeatedly talking about past mistakes or the wrongful actions of those who may have hurt you, or excessive dependencies.
7. Never blow little problems out of proportion. Let them go and trust that God will take care of the circumstances.
8. Avoid, as much as possible, outside influences that can bring you down, such as bad news shows, songs with hateful lyrics, or depressing articles or Internet sites.
9. Don't allow those individuals who are constantly complaining and fault-finding make you feel guilt because you do not do what they want. Their manipulation can slow you down and zap your energy.

The negative attitudes and conduct of others can drag you down quickly, so use caution with whom you trust. Impostors can tear up your dreams and their wrong thoughts, actions, and attitudes may come disguised in a very clever package. And, if left to remain, they can destroy all of the loveliness of life. A highly regarded entrepreneur said to me once, "I trust everyone I meet for the first five minutes, and then I let my heart tell me if I should continue."

*"As a face is reflected in water, so the
heart reflects the real person."*

PROVERBS 27:19, NLT

A businesswoman from the East Coast told me that some years ago she had started a business with a small group of people and invested a large sum of money. After a short time, she realized the individuals she'd begun the enterprise with were not capable of good, honest dealings. And the venture she'd assumed she would be participating in, as well as sharing the profits, was being mismanaged. She ignored the questionable behavior for a while. But subsequently, her business associates took control of the operation and forced her out. The dispirited woman was full of anxiety, unable to sleep, and racked by deep depression. Nothing seemed to console her. "Finally," she said, "I came to the conclusion that my worry, fear, and resentment were causing my suffering."

She continued, "I prayed and put the whole matter into the hands of God and let it all go. Soon, I was able to forgive, and ceased worrying and resenting my former business partners. My health immediately improved and I had the strength to start again . . . this time with increased wisdom and discernment."

Develop a network of encouraging friends and caring relatives who will provide companionship, listen, and simply be there when you need support.

As we draw closer to God through prayer and reading His word, He will reveal the marvels of His good judgment and the wonders of His wisdom. And He will give knowledge and insight, so that we can live safely, victoriously, and joyfully.

DAY FOUR:

PERSISTENCE CAN SUDDENLY PAY OFF.

"I have fought the good fight, I have finished the race,
I have kept the faith."
2 TIMOTHY 4:7, NIV

The first time you tried, you hit a bump in the road . . . *and you kept on going.*

The second time you attempted to go forth, a huge boulder was blocking your path . . . *and you went around it.*

The third time you made an effort . . . someone purposely held out their foot and tripped you . . . *but you stood up again.*

The fourth time you endeavored, nothing seemed to be happening . . . *however, you worked and waited patiently for your situation to turn around.*

The fifth time you tried, although tired, you prayed to God for strength . . . *and persevered.*

And God took the impossible and transformed it into a miracle . . . *and you made it to your destination!*

Do you accept "no" too easily? Do you believe that "no" is final? Do you think that things will always be the way they are now, not recognizing that situations can change?

The first book of Samuel, chapter 1, of the Old Testament demonstrates the perseverance of a woman named Hannah. Hannah ardently desired to have a child, so she took her petition to God. But, month after month, year after year, God was silent toward her request.

Hannah could have easily given up and, as the years passed, succumbed to being bitter and resentful toward God, for "the Lord had closed her womb" (1 Samuel 1:5). Instead, Hannah persevered in her quest. Others mocked, ridiculed, and taunted Hannah because she was childless. However, this humble woman of prayer persistently kept pouring her heart out to God. Hannah promised God that if she had a son, she would give him back to God's service. And she didn't abandon hope, for she had great faith that God had the power to alter her condition and help her bring forth a child.

Wondrously, God did answer Hannah's persistent prayers with a son, whom she named Samuel. "For this child I prayed, and the Lord has granted me my petition that I made to Him" (1 Samuel 1:27). And Hannah was quick to thank and praise God. Moreover, she was abundantly fruitful in her life, as God blessed Hannah with three more sons and two daughters (1 Samuel 1:17, ESV).

"Perseverance [is the] secret of all triumphs."

Victor Hugo

Today, I want you to give yourself the persistence test: Ask yourself these six questions and jot down "yes," "no," or "maybe" next to the question.

1. Do I believe in myself?
2. Am I living a balanced life, via family, faith, health, and career?
3. Do I know exactly for what I am striving?
4. Is my faith strong?

5. Do I have the determination to see my aspirations through to completion?
6. Is there a good support system around me?

If you answered "maybe" or "no" to any of these questions, perhaps that is the area in which you need to work. If you answered "yes" to these questions, you are well on your way to success.

Do you know that many of us give up just when we are about to accomplish something great? Therefore, keep at it, give it one more try, and don't stop now. Keep praying. Your miracle may be right around the next corner.

Memorize this mantra: "By the inch your goals are a cinch." Then, follow this act: Break your goals down into smaller tasks to make them more manageable.

I recall a memorable moment last fall, when my family and I were hiking up a long mountain trail. After about an hour, my middle daughter, Gabriella, asked, "What kind of path is this, Mommy? It is so bumpy, rough, and full of large rocks." Quickly, I replied, "Just keep on climbing over the bumps, carry on, just persist in climbing, and soon we will arrive at the top."

Life holds the same principle. Frequently, we must try again and again, repeatedly, before we succeed in an endeavor. Perhaps we have to submit a proposal 20 times before it is accepted. Or struggle for years with that bad habit, prior to it being conquered. Possibly, we have had countless delays and setbacks before we achieved a goal. And maybe we had to remind ourselves hundreds of times that we are "worthy," "strong," and "loved," before it sank into our heart and we really believed it. But I know you have what it takes to persevere, determinedly stand up to any obstacles, and prevail over them.

Remember, with every "no" you are closer to a "yes."

When I was growing up, we had a dog named Frenchie. He was a small, seven-pound French poodle, but he had a huge bark. If anyone knocked on our door or even walked by the house, Frenchie would start barking ferociously. His size didn't matter. If he faced a situation that appeared improbable, even though he was so small, this little poodle did not back down and run away. Even though he had hindrances, he utilized what he had, stood his ground, and persevered.

In the same way, if you have a challenge, do not yield or pull back, discouraged. Just as it was for Frenchie, it is not your size, limitations, or obstacles in your way that count; it is your faith, your attitude, strength of mind, and fortitude that will bring you success and fulfillment.

Despite the odds, anything in life is achievable. Recall the saying, "Where there is a will, there is way." You have the will, the determination, and the staying power to win, because you are much stronger than the challenges before you. When everything seems to be going wrong, and you don't know where to turn next, while some people say, "It's time to give up," that's the moment to trust God, work even harder, and persist onward.

Think about it like this: There were two builders who wanted to construct a house. They purchased one-acre lots next to each other, drew up their home plans, excavated the land, and poured the foundation. However, a storm came, with wind and rain. The first builder waited and waited and did nothing. The second builder carried on building his house. He did not wait for perfect conditions; he didn't talk about never-ending problems or allow obstacles out of his control to stop him. He built his house anyway.

Treat yourself lovingly. Give yourself a gift, such as a new outfit, a manicure, or a celebratory dinner out with your family, after you complete a certain goal.

What am I asking you to do today? The storm may be furious; the wind may be raging, but build anyway; don't concede defeat, but instead, go forward with thoughts of victory. Stand up to your obstacles, and soon, those obstacles will be crumbled and removed.

Scripture says in Proverbs 1:31 (NLV), "So, they will eat the fruit of their own way . . ." In other words, change your words and attitude from doubt to faith, from inaction to action, from idleness to persevering, and positive things can begin to materialize.

One way to do this is to release your strength with the words you speak. For instance, if you are having monetary trouble and you have been saying, "It's hopeless; I'll never get out of debt." Or, if you're going through a difficult breakup, and you've been uttering to friends, "It's too late for me now, no one will ever love me again," you can trade these disempowering statements for words that will give you the strength to persevere.

For the next two hours, I'd like you to replace any negative talk with optimistic declarations such as, "God is at work in my life," "Something good is going to happen for my family," and "I am on the threshold of unparalleled success." After the two hours, ask yourself, "Do I feel better?" Now, continue this exercise for the rest of the day and realize that what you say can change the course of your destiny.

I have heard it said, "Most people look up and admire the stars, but a champion climbs a mountain and grabs one . . ." You are a champion; you have extraordinary gifts to offer to this world . . . So keep climbing.

Day Five:

If you take the first step, God will do the rest.

*"It is God who arms me with strength and
makes my way perfect."*

PSALM 18:32, NIV

Every once in a while, I glance up at a quote that I have posted in my office. The words are from author Napoleon Hill. His motivating passage helps me persist and take another step past obstacles and toward my goals:

Before success comes in any man's life, he is sure to meet with much temporary defeat and, perhaps, some failure. When defeat overtakes a man, the easiest and most logical thing to do is to quit. That is exactly what the majority of men do.

More than five hundred of the most successful men this country has ever known told the author their greatest success came just one step beyond the point at which defeat had overtaken them.

Recently, I went on a business trip to QVC Television in Pennsylvania, and I thought about the life of entrepreneur Milton S. Hershey. As I drove my car through the charming town of Lancaster, I recalled a book I had read years before about

226

Hershey's path to success, which was paved with stumbling blocks and pitfalls.

Hershey was a farm boy who left school in the fourth grade and then apprenticed for a printer who published a newspaper. He was not keen on that line of work, and soon left. Thereafter, he started an apprenticeship for a candy-maker, and found that he had a natural talent for the "sweet" profession. After a few years, young Hershey decided to go out on his own. His limited funds and limited formal education did not stop him from following his vision, and thus, he began a candy company. Yet, after some time, it failed. Hershey tried again, and determinedly founded another candy enterprise. It was unsuccessful, too.

Lacking resources and almost bankrupt, courageously, Hershey didn't yield. Refusing to falter in the face of adversity, he looked into the future. Working hard, Hershey persevered, and with the important lessons he had learned, he kept moving forward toward his utmost goals.

A turning point came in Hershey's life when he utilized a unique caramel recipe upon which he had stumbled during his earlier days, and he launched the Lancaster Caramel Company. Before long, the business became a great success.

However, through his experiences, Hershey astutely believed that chocolate products would appeal to the masses. Through trial and error, he worked tirelessly at perfecting a delicious milk chocolate recipe. Subsequently, he sold the Caramel Company for a large sum of money in order to devote all his time to realizing his dream of manufacturing and distributing chocolate, while giving generously to philanthropic causes. Today, "Hershey" is a household name.

In view of Milton Hershey's story, here are some questions for discussion:

✧ Have you allowed past setbacks to weaken you and prevent you from pressing on to fulfill the dreams of your heart?

✧ Are you willing to acknowledge and address the areas with which you need help?

✧ How can a person keep going when things get tough?

Like Milton Hershey, take one more step forward. God can do the impossible for you. And so, begin to weave the life of your dreams and the thread will come.

You can rise above anything that happens to you if you have the right perspective. I'd like you to sit quietly for five minutes and consider the circumstance which you are facing. Now, ask yourself: "What would God say to me right now?" Listen for His answer, think carefully, and then: Believe in your God-given purpose!

1. Keep your mind open to fresh, positive thoughts.
2. If you make mistakes along the way, adjust your future actions based on what happened in the past.
3. See the glass as half full, and try again if you hit a stumbling block.
4. Have confidence that the little steps you take will add up to a great, big blessing.

Keep in mind, the situation which you are confronted with right now may help you to develop a stronger faith in God, lead you to meet great people, put you in the position to meet the needs of others, or inspire you to live a better life.

Yes, maybe your dream is taking a long time to come to pass, and at times you may not know if you have the strength to continue. Possibly, you've tried and failed. Or perhaps, you are feeling dismayed by discouragements, and you're ready to throw up your hands and say, "I give up."

But no matter what you may be facing, keep the big picture of your life in the forefront of your mind. With perseverance, problems can be turned around to your advantage. And an end of the road can lead to a new beginning.

Picture your life in ten years. Is what you are doing now an indication that you will be happy, purposeful, and fulfilled? If not, adjust your priorities.

Great opportunities can be concealed as obstacles. Blessings may come disguised as trials. And something good will come from the adversity you now face. Behind a mask of adversity, God was shaping Moses to stand before Pharaoh and say, "Let my people go, that they may serve me." For years, in the walls of a prison cell, the Apostle Paul authored parts of the New Testament. And suffering great losses, Job learned to trust God under all conditions.

Because of his perseverance, Moses led the people out of Israel. The Apostle Paul's influence has been greater than that of any other apostle, as he wrote much of the Bible's New Testament. And Job was given back twice what he lost.

You have the potential to accomplish great things. Hence, don't turn back now because you are focused on past mishaps or obstacles. You could be close to your breakthrough! Primarily, be true to yourself by following what is in your heart and what you believe to be true, rather than acting against your better judgment or principles. For when you are true to yourself, you will nourish your motivation to persevere. Have faith that, with God, you can overcome the seemingly insurmountable odds.

✧ Begin to implement a new concept.

✧ Think out-of-the-box.

✧ Make another phone call.

- ✧ Try different directions than the ones you have taken in the past. You may discover hidden gifts.

- ✧ Network through other people. Tap into your contact list, e-mail them, and ask for their help.

- ✧ Follow up on any lead. Success is not always necessarily where you expect to find it.

> *"In the confrontation between the stream*
> *and the rock, the stream always wins—not*
> *through strength but by perseverance."*
>
> H. Jackson Brown

Today is a pivotal day. Let go of the failures, setbacks, and unfair situations of the past. God has a bigger purpose in mind for you, so just keep taking steps ahead and trust in Him, because He is arranging situations for you! Just beyond the difficulty awaits victory.

> *Thus, understanding God's purpose, pick up*
> *your Bible and read God's word to . . .*
> *"Know it in your mind.*
> *Stow it in your heart.*
> *Show it in your life.*
> *And sow it to the world."*
>
> Author unknown

The possibilities for your life are endless, so step out boldly and let God lead you. This is the moment you have been waiting for; it is your time, it's your chance to shine.

Day six:

Reach forth with fortitude and take your gifts out into the world.

"Whatever you do, work at it with all your heart, as working for the Lord, not for men, since you know that you will receive an inheritance from the Lord as a reward."
Colossians 3:23-24, NIV

In the mid-60s, a baby boy was born without a right hand. As he grew up, this boy came to love to play sports and particularly baseball. And at an early age, he refused to let his limitation pigeonhole him, so he decided to ignore his disability. Thus, he was diligent, worked hard, and trained relentlessly, and even pretended to be some of his favorite pitchers.

This boy developed extraordinary hand-eye coordination and quick reflexes, which allowed him to do with one hand what others did with two hands. He played Little League, but people would tell him that his playing days would probably end there. Yet, this youngster disregarded the skeptics. He used his keen mind to imagine himself becoming a successful athlete. He planned, he dreamed. Allowing his imagination to bring him new insights and ideas, he made the choice to persist, taking action to formulate his dreams into a reality. And his tenacity won out.

Jim Abbott went on to a successful career pitching major league baseball. In an interview, Abbott said, "No matter where the road takes you, don't give up until you know in your heart you have done everything you possibly could to make your dreams come true. You owe nothing to disability, ignore it. When you fail, get back up and try again. Leave no room for an excuse."

Today, begin by asking yourself, "How can I make the best use of what God has given to me?" "If I could have anything in life, what would it be?" Let your imagination go, and dream. Do not count yourself out. Life gave Jim Abbott what he asked of it, because he was willing to reach for it with fortitude. And now, he is an inspiring role model to people worldwide.

To shorten the distance between perseverance and achievement, learn from successful people. Has what you want to do been done before? Well, if someone else can, you certainly can achieve your goals, too.

1. Talk to a person who has accomplished what you'd like to do.
2. Ask them, "How did you get where you are today? And request their advice, inquiring, "What steps can I take to succeed in my endeavor?"
3. Gain knowledge from the successes, as well as the mistakes, of others.

> *"That some achieve great success, is proof to all that others can achieve it as well."*
>
> ABRAHAM LINCOLN

I recall one afternoon when I was at a book signing at a floral and gift shop in Rhode Island autographing copies of my new book. After the signing, I was talking to some of my readers, and a woman shared a simple story with me about an experience that had had a profound impact on her life.

She shared that she is an avid gardener, and that one day she was planting roses in her garden and a bee was buzzing around her. "I ignored it for a while, and then brushed the insect aside with my hand," the woman declared. "But the bee returned," she said, grinning and shaking her head from side to side. "So I tried to swat it away again," she explained. "Yet, the bee came back."

While listening to her, I curiously began to wonder where she was going with this story. Certainly, she had my full attention.

Next, the woman told me that the bee landed on a flower right beside to her, and she noticed that one of its wings was injured. Fascinated, she bent over to get a closer look. "How could this bee fly with just one good wing?" she asked herself.

Nevertheless, the bee overlooked its seemingly hopeless situation, and persisted. The bee took to the air unflinchingly, flying unhindered from flower to flower, with only one good wing.

"Soon, the bee left my garden, though it left a lasting effect in my heart," the woman confided. Thereafter, she leaned close to me and said, "Through the years, remembering that little bee's persistence helped me to overcome extreme adversity and hardships."

Listen to stories, read literature, and watch movies and documentaries about stories of inspiration. Select those with strong, uplifting themes which can nurture your mind and spirit. The tales of true champions and their persistence can offer sterling examples for you to gain insight from and follow in your own life.

God deserves your best. So, don't live beneath your capabilities, taking the easy way out, the convenient road of least resistance. Be determined to live the best life that you can. When you settle for the status quo, you can lose your motivation, enthusiasm, and passion. Plus, the extreme good you can do for others and the world around you can go unmet. The prize is worth the price and the rewards will be well worth it!

> *God loves you and He wants you to succeed. It's not like the Olympics, with only one gold medal for each event; God is for everyone, we can all be winners . . . and He is there rooting for you!*

Once, I heard somebody inquire, "If you could hear God whispering in your ear, *'I am with you,' 'Be of good courage,' 'Persevere,' 'Keep going'* and *'I am directing your path,'* would you give up?" Often times, God has a handful of new blessings for us, yet we are stuck in the hurts of the long ago, or held back by regrets or some limitation. As a result, we can become so absorbed in the darkness that, like quicksand, it can completely consume us.

The Apostle Paul told Timothy that "words of faith" nourish, but idle words starve the spirit and make it weak (1 Timothy 4:6-7). Paul was encouraging Timothy not to give up but, instead, to spread hope throughout the world. Thoughts and words of doubt, discouragement, or fear, as Paul mentioned, can prevent us from receiving all God has for us.

Consider what Scripture tells us:

- ✧ "Life and death are in the power of the tongue" (Proverbs 18:21, HCSB).
- ✧ "Whoso keepeth his mouth and his tongue keepeth his soul from troubles" (Proverbs 21:23).

✧ "For out of the abundance of the heart the mouth speaketh" (Matthew 12:34-37).

Therefore, begin today to speak forth hopeful, victorious, life-affirming words about yourself, and extend positive words and encouragement to others. Scripture also states, "Let us hold fast the confession of our hope without wavering, for He who promised is faithful" (Hebrews 10:23, NASB). Our declarations are our "confessions," for the words we express can influence the way we feel and act, as well as allow us to alter conditions in one direction or the other. What comes out of our mouth determines our attitude and our outlook on life.

To build your fortitude, keep a stack of inspirational quotations by your nightstand to read before bedtime and fuel your motivation. Here are a few terrific quotes to get you started:

✧ When the world says, "Give up," hope whispers, "Try it one more time."

✧ "There will come a time when you believe everything is finished. That will be the beginning." —Louis L'Amour

✧ "The greatest oak was once a little nut that held its ground." —Author Unknown

✧ "It always seems impossible until it's done." —Nelson Mandela

✧ "Much rain wears the marble." —Shakespeare

I believe you cannot fail if you persevere. In your mind's eye, visualize the great Creator of the Universe going before you, standing behind you and guiding every step you take. And listen intently, for God is saying to you today, *"I am with you," "Be of good courage," "Persevere," "Keep going,"* and *"I am directing your path."* Then, go out each day and share your incredible gifts with the world.

DAY SEVEN:

REGARDLESS OF CHALLENGES, YOU CAN LIVE YOUR DREAM.

"I know your works. Behold, I have set before you an open door,
which no one is able to shut. I know that you have
but little power, and yet you have kept my word and
have not denied my name."
REVELATION 3:8, ESV

A poor soul knelt and bowed his head at God's footstool to confess:
   "I failed," the man cried.
   But the Master said,
   "Son, thou didst thy best . . . that is success."
   I wanted to share with you this sweet verse of poetry, which a dear reader sent to me, for I believe it holds within it great meaning and truth.
   The highest goal and greatest reward exist *in the effort* you make to achieve your full potential. What you put forth into your life—the quality, the joy, the faith, the love, the enthusiasm, the courage, the foresight—determines your success. There's no such word as *fail* if you sincerely try.
   There may have been countless setbacks, obstacles, and honest mistakes made along your pathway. Maybe you've encountered

one slipup after another. Perhaps, you've made an error in judgment. Or a mistake in trusting someone, and they deliberately tried to hurt you. Now, you're disheartened, worn out, and ready to relinquish your utmost dreams and goals for your future.

Friends, do not be afraid of making mistakes.

"But," you might utter, "Nothing is going my way. What if I try and fall short again?"

Well, I say, "Forget past setbacks and then try one more time!"

Anne Morrow Lindbergh, beloved author, and wife of aviator Charles Lindbergh, wrote, "It takes as much courage to have tried and failed as it does to have tried and succeeded." Set your sights high, far above the ordinary. Always be yourself, think your own great thoughts, and don't run with the crowd. Have a resolute aim. Be a person of honor. Strive for excellence in all that you undertake, and embrace every opportunity. You have potential far beyond what you think is possible. Therefore, never stop trying to be the best that you can be.

> *"Perseverance is a great element of success. If you knock long enough and loud enough at the gate, you are sure to wake up somebody."*
>
> HENRY WADSWORTH LONGFELLOW

I know that God has a wonderful plan for your life. So make Him your highest priority. Each day: 1) Love God; 2) Seek God; 3) Honor God; 4) Please God; and 5) Thank God. He has not brought you this far to let you fall down now. Don't quit; keep searching for the open window. There is no obstacle that is too big for God to turn around for your greater good. That's why you can put your trust and confidence in Him. And that trust and joyful expectation can transform impossibilities into realities.

Recorded in all four gospels—Matthew (14:16-21), Mark

(6:35-44), Luke (9:12-17), and John (6:5-14)—is the account of Jesus feeding the multitudes. The story goes that Jesus took five small loaves of bread and two fish, looked up into Heaven, blessed the food, broke the loaves, and gave them to His disciples to set before the people. Then, Jesus divided the two fish among them all. The food was multiplied, and all 5,000 men, as well as women and children, ate until they were full. Furthermore, there was even food left over, which tells me: if we believe and genuinely continue to try, no matter how meager our resources, God will certainly meet our needs.

Rather than giving up, build yourself up by praying The Prayer of Jabez each morning: "Oh, that you would bless me and enlarge my territory! Let your hand be with me, and keep me from harm so that I will be free from pain" (1 Chronicles 4:10, NIV). The name Jabez means "he causes pain" so, at his birth, Jabez was labeled with "hurt and sorrow." In his time, names were seen as prophetic, often having a great hand in defining a person's future. But Jabez grew to be a righteous man of prayer who believed fervently in the power of God. He put himself unconditionally in God's hands and wanted God's blessings on his life to be fulfilled. When Jabez prayed this prayer, God "granted him that which he requested." If God gave Jebez what he asked for, He can do the same for you.

When you hit a stumbling block, as we all do, I'd like you to move boldly past it. If God presents you with a dream and a vision for your future, never let it go. Attempt to achieve it. Similar to a puppy holding on to a shoe in his mouth, adhere to your goals; grasp hold of them and, akin to that persistent puppy, refuse to let them go!

Life has two rules. The first rule is to never give up.
The second rule is to remember the first rule.

Invariably, the most persistent people are the most successful. So act. Proceed forward. Make things happen in your life, instead of just sitting back and waiting for something to come to you. God sends food to the tiniest of birds, yet He does not place the food into the birds' nests. The birds must go out and find it. Likewise, with self-reliance, put forth the effort, following your aspirations with tenacity of purpose.

Once I heard a simple story about a teenage boy who attended a traveling country fair. While he was in the audience watching a horse show, this boy heard the ringmaster offer ten dollars to the person who could ride one of his unruly horses around the ring and not get thrown off. A number of seasoned horsemen tried to ride the horse, with no success, and gave up their attempts.

Thereafter, this teenager stood up and said, "I would like to try." Although he had never ridden a horse before, he climbed onto the large animal and rode halfway around the ring. But then he was thrown off.

However, failure did not faze this boy. So, rather than giving up, he went back to the starting gate, mounted the horse, and tried again. Yet, a second time, he fell off the horse.

The audience stared in amazement at the boy's tenacity, as he brushed the dirt off of himself and exclaimed, "Let me try once more."

This time, with the lessons learned from his previous attempts, the boy hung on, clinging to the animal with all of his might. And he successfully made it around the ring and won the prize.

My good friend from exercise class recently told me, "What you are is a result of what you have done. What you *become* is a result of what you do right now!"

Spend a few moments alone, look in the mirror, and ask yourself, "Should I stop pursuing something that I really desire, because I've made some slipups?" "How would I feel a year or two from now if I quit?"

Regardless of mistakes in the past, please continue to try, to do and to be your very best. Make the most of yourself and live for the purpose for which you were created. God has bestowed upon you a sacred trust. He has given you exceptional dreams and extraordinary abilities, with which to bless the world. Use your gifts for God's glory and the betterment of mankind and you will reap eternal dividends.

And that . . . I consider is the greatest success of all.

Window Seven

Share Your Strength with Others

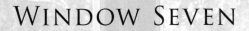

"Give a man a fish and you feed him for a day.
Teach a man to fish and you feed him for a lifetime."
Chinese proverb

DAY ONE:

LEARN TO OVERCOME WITH GOD'S STRENGTH, NOT JUST YOUR OWN.

"But now, O Lord, You are our Father; we are the clay, and You our potter; and all we are the work of Your hand."
ISAIAH 64:8, NKJV

There is a cute tale about a couple who were shopping at an antique shop. As they looked around the old country store, they glanced up on a shelf and saw an exquisite teapot.

As the woman reached for it, the teapot began to talk. "I did not always look like this," said the teapot. "There was a time that I used to be a cold lump of clay and no one wanted me. I was depressed, disheartened, and unappealing. But then, one day, a potter came along, and with his mighty hands, he began to shape me and form me."

The teapot continued, "As he was molding me, it was uncomfortable, so I told the potter to leave me alone, but he grinned and uttered, 'Not yet.'

"After that, the potter put me on a wheel, holding me in a secure position with his firm but tender and unyielding hands. As he began to spin me around, I yelled, 'Potter, what are you doing? That hurts.' The potter carried on, forming me into a one-of-a-kind, unique shape.

"Then, he put me in a hot furnace and I shouted, 'Leave me alone; this is terrible. Let me out.' And the potter replied, 'Not yet.'

"Next, he put me on the shelf and I thought it was finally over. But again, the potter picked me up and started to paint me with a gluey, smelly paint. And I didn't like it; I was so upset that I became bitter and resentful.

"Last of all, he put me into a sweltering oven. I was very angry and roared, 'Potter, I cannot handle it. Leave me alone; this hurts.' He said, 'Not yet.'

"A few days later, when he was finished, the potter handed me a mirror. When I looked into that mirror, I couldn't believe how much I had changed. Completely transformed, I felt valuable, important, and wanted. Something wonderful had come from all that suffering. For all along, the potter knew my true worth and, through the tribulations, he was forming me and my character."

The Bible says that "God is the potter and we are the clay." God uses the struggles just as the potter, with his skillful hands, squeezes the clay. And, like the potter, God is transforming us little by little, forming and refining us into something beautiful, for His good purpose.

"And yet, O Lord, you are our Father. We are the clay, and you are the potter. We all are formed by your hand"
(Isaiah 64:8, NLT).

"The precious sons of Zion, comparable to fine gold, how are they esteemed as earthen pitchers, the work of the hands of the potter!"
(Lamentations 4:2).

". . . saith the Lord, 'Behold, as the clay is in the potter's hand, so are ye in mine hand, O house of Israel'"
(Jeremiah 18:6).

"And the Lord God formed man of the dust of the ground, and breathed into his nostrils the breath of life; and man became a living soul"

(Genesis 2:7).

Are you struggling through a circumstance and grasping for answers? How should you act in response to what you are facing? Respond with faith and allow God to do His work and develop you to your fullest and highest potential. Think about it this way: Every experience is trying to teach you something that you can carry with you for your entire life.

Take a blank sheet of notepaper and draw a line down the middle. On one side, note the stumbling blocks that have been placed in your way in the past. And on the other side of the paper, list what you learned from the experience. For example, when you had to wait for something you wanted, did you develop patience? When you were pushed down by a hurtful person yet got back up and tried again, did you discover the important trait of persistence? If you didn't understand "why a situation was happening," did you learn to trust God? And later understood "why," when things fell into place? This assessment can help you gain some insight into challenging circumstances.

Yes, it is the power and strength that comes from God's mighty hand that will hold and carry you through any situation. So, if you feel as though you're in the "molding" process, keep these thoughts with you to read during the course of your day for self-empowerment and reinforcement:

✧ God placed unlimited possibilities within you, and before long, they will be brought out.

✧ You possess marvelous attributes that are increasing daily, so keep working and striving toward your heart's dream.

✧ With every difficulty, you are gaining strength and skills that will be utilized in the future.

✧ A new set of blessings are ahead, awakening you to your greatest achievements.

✧ The happiest moments for you and your loved ones are still to come.

✧ God is transforming conditions now to your best advantage.

> *"For the eyes of the Lord run to and fro throughout the whole earth to show Himself strong in behalf of those whose hearts are blameless toward Him."*
>
> 2 CHRONICLES 16:9, AMP

A Missouri reader of my column advised, "Let us be patient and pray, being assured that God uses our tribulations to teach us to rely on Him, and prepares us for greater accomplishments ahead."

Do you remember the lesson of the butterfly? For it is in the struggle that we learn and grow strong, like the silken cocoon that the butterfly must break out of to freedom.

Once a scientist watched this struggle, decided to help, and snipped the cocoon just a little. The butterfly popped out easily, but never flew.

Accordingly, the cocoon offers just enough resistance so that, in

246

struggling to escape, life-giving fluids are forced into the butterfly's wings and they are strengthened. The butterfly is then able to break free and soar joyfully into the warm, fragrant summer breeze. It is through the long, hard struggle that the butterfly gains enough power to fly.

Today, if you are being tried and tested, I'd like you to do as it says in Mark 6:31: "Come ye yourselves apart . . . and rest for a while." Regroup, reflect, and simply "lay low" for a bit. Embrace a faith-filled, hopeful outlook, look up to the sky, and say, "Lord, help me to learn what you are teaching me." Ask God to guide you and express gratitude for the person that you are, cultivating an appreciation for your strengths and gifts. And then, go forward with a new focus.

If you trust God and have the right attitude, He will somehow turn your situation around and you will come out of it successfully. As a result, don't be afraid if God wants to stretch your abilities and your horizons in the divine plan that He has already set up for your life. Just stay the course with Him, for His eyes and attention are always on you.

DAY TWO:

A LITTLE LOVE AND KINDNESS GO A LONG WAY.

"Be perfect, be of good comfort, be of one mind, live in peace;
and the God of love and peace shall be with you."

2 CORINTHIANS 13:11

Last night, our three daughters wanted to prepare dinner. So into the kitchen they went. From the living room, my husband and I heard them stirring, peeling, and preparing the feast. Not sure what was going on, I asked, "What ingredients are you using?"

Giggling, our oldest daughter said, "We are putting *love* in the meatloaf." Then, as our middle daughter was setting the table, she called out, "We put *love* in the potatoes." And thereafter our youngest followed suit saying, "We put *love* in everything."

"For beautiful eyes, look for the good in others; for beautiful lips, speak only words of kindness; and for poise, walk with the knowledge that you are never alone."

AUDREY HEPBURN

That is what we all should do . . . *"Put love in everything!"*

If we all took on this attitude, think about how much we could accomplish.

248

Let's put *love* into and let peace illuminate our homes. Let's put *love* into our relationships, and *love* in our vocations. We must treat people with appreciation, respect, and kindness, being an example of God's love. And we must look for ways to be a blessing to others, reaching our hand out in love, to care for, to share, and to give support. This is how we grow and stay strong, for we are more powerful together than we are alone.

What are your greatest strengths? What comes easy for you? Take a moment and jot down characteristics and skills that you do well. Then, access those incredible qualities and share the strengths you've discovered with the world.

✦ If someone you know is discouraged, share stories of how you've prevailed over challenging circumstances in your own life.

✦ If there's a need in your community, give your time and energy freely to the cause.

✦ Be kind to the environment. Avoid littering and treat the natural world with loving care.

✦ Show love to animals and volunteer at a shelter.

✦ Pick up the phone and call a friend who may be disheartened, and contribute your knowledge and accumulated wisdom.

✦ Maybe you know a person who needs a job. Think of some of your contacts, send a note or e-mail, and give them a good recommendation.

One act of love can open up a whole new world of awareness. Let's open our Bibles and look up John 2:1-11 for an example of love. It tells us that Jesus, His mother, Mary, and the disciples were guests at a wedding in Cana. The wine ran out, and through the urging and expectation of His mother, Jesus took the six water pots filled to the brim with water, and He turned them into wine.

However, He created not just any wine, but the finest of wines. Jesus brought something new and better to the guests at the wedding, showing that He was filled with love, kindness, and the joy of life.

So, add light to someone else's life with a word of praise or a thoughtful gesture. Let us make the way easier for others, by helping them whenever we can. Be happy for other people's successes. Rejoicing in someone else's accomplishments not only reveals a confident, strong person, but also indicates that they are worthy of great success themselves. These confident, strong individuals understand the principle that, collectively, we can do so much good.

"Snowflakes are one of nature's most fragile things, but just look what they can do when they stick together."

VISTA M. KELLY

I read an article once about Olympic swimming medalist Dana Torres. While at the 2008 Olympic Games in Beijing, just before she was to compete in the women's 50-meter freestyle semifinals, she stopped to help another competitor whose swimsuit was ripped. Then, when the participant's swimsuit could not be fixed, Torres went a step further and asked the officials to delay the race, so the other athlete could quickly change.

Torres did not think of her own warm-up or her focus just before the competition, nor her years of grueling work and rigorous training. Her thought was to help her competitor, an athlete from Sweden that she barely even knew. The 2008 Olympic Games were most likely Torres's last chance to win a gold metal. However, in an act of selflessness, exemplifying good sportsmanship and consideration for others, she put another competitor first, before her own ambition.

Torres's unselfish act of love speaks volumes to us, even more than her extraordinary athletic capabilities. This reminds me of the Bible verse that states: "For with the measure you use, it will be measured back to you" (Luke 6:38, NIV). And, "Cast thy bread upon the water for thou shall find it after many days" (Ecclesiastes 11:1). Offer the best you have, for whatever we send out will return back and what we do for others will eventually be done to us.

A Missouri reader wrote, "I have always tried to live life by the premise of, 'Treat others the way you would wish for them to treat you.' My mother also shares this philosophy . . . she was the wise woman who instilled that value deep within my moral fabric."

For some time now, I've been corresponding with a woman who is battling a long illness. Yet, through it all, she has drawn closer to God, her character has been strengthened, and her testimony of overcoming severe obstacles has helped countless people.

"I have learned," she wrote, "that the goal of life is to grow in character and to help others." This woman chooses to get her mind off of her problems by giving out love, and has stated that her own life has been thus immensely enriched. She has said she started the process by simply smiling at those she came into contact with, and facing the day with a reverence for the many opportunities it holds to assist those in need.

Let's do what this reader suggests: as we go about our day, put on a cheerful countenance, a happy expression. Keep your mind in good spirits, because where your mind goes, your hands, your feet, and your actions will follow.

We should never neglect the little things, because the smallest thing a person does in love can make the biggest impact.

✧ Hug your child and let the embrace last longer than usual.

✧ Wake up early and watch a magnificent sunrise with your loved ones.

✧ Send a handwritten card to those who have positively influenced your life.

✧ Hold hands with those you love.

✧ Write, "I love you" on sticky notes and place them in unexpected places around the house, in your child's lunchbox or spouse's computer bag.

✧ Surprise someone with a bouquet of fresh flowers.

At a set time every morning and evening, take five minutes to close your eyes, reflect on others, and wish them well.

God wants to give you the very best. Love others and delight yourself in Him, and you will feel like the boy that gave his five loaves and two fish to Jesus, and then stood back in amazement at what He did with them. Jesus multiplied, and multiplied. So always give your love to God and live a life that is pleasing to Him. And then, watch what He will do for you.

DAY THREE:

SETTING A GOOD EXAMPLE BENEFITS GENERATIONS TO COME.

"And you yourself must be an example to them by doing good works of every kind. Let everything you do reflect the integrity and seriousness of your teaching."
TITUS 2:7, NLT

One afternoon, a young man went to see a well-respected executive in the community and asked for his advice. This young man had a newfound invention, and he needed funds to get his business off the ground.

The executive listened carefully to the young entrepreneur's presentation and without hesitation he said, "I will help you."

Stunned, the young man asked, "What did I do to deserve this kindness?"

Gently, the executive responded, "You didn't do anything. But years ago, when I was trying to get started in a career, your grandfather prayed for and encouraged me."

The executive explained, "I came from a poor family and when I was a child I lost both my parents. Downtrodden and disregarded, with little education and not much hope, I wanted to give up on life. Then, I met your grandfather. And I will never forget how considerate and generous he was to me." Then, he exclaimed, "I am helping you now, because of your grandfather." This grandfather's generosity and selflessness had an impact on the executive, and his grandson's life was helped because of one man's goodness and the life that he chose to live.

Nobel Prize winner Albert Schweitzer wrote, "Example is not the main thing in influencing others, it is the only thing." There is a transcendent power in setting an example. Not only does the example teach, but it is also the most prominent thing that others see. Firsthand observations promptly stay in our memory, and subconsciously we can be positively transformed by good examples.

Give some thought to these questions: What examples are you passing down to the next generation? How can you accumulate blessings for your children, grandchildren, their children, and even total strangers? How are your personal choices affecting our young people? We don't live our life solely unto ourselves.

Today, ask a young person what they remember most about a relative or person they knew who passed away. Their answer may cause you to realize the impact your decisions of today will have on tomorrow. Always be a fine example—the rewards are well worth it.

Next, I'd like you to think about what you can do to impact

those who will go ahead of you. Here are a couple of ideas to get you started:

1. Keep your promises.
2. Be happy and have a positive outlook.
3. Help a neighbor with outside chores or household responsibilities regularly.
4. Bring out the good side in all conversations.
5. Pass down your wisdom, your faith in God, and a hard work ethic to the youngsters in your life.
6. Be honest in all dealings.

I once read a news story depicting how Josh Ferrin of Utah had just purchased his first home. After the closing, Josh walked through the front door and began looking around. Then, he went into the garage and noticed a small door in the ceiling. So he got a ladder and climbed up, and there he saw a black metal box. Inside the box were bags of money and some memorabilia.

Immediately, Josh closed the box and called his wife to tell her what he had found in their new home. Since the original homeowner

Dr. Samuel Johnson once said, "We cannot look into the hearts of men, but their actions are open to observation." For when we live a life of faith and integrity, make good choices, assist those in need, and offer selfless acts of kindness, we leave behind a legacy. We may never know the long-term consequences of how that good deed affects future generations, but it profoundly will.

had passed away in November, Josh called the homeowner's son and returned the $45,000 dollars in cash that he had found.

Josh said to a reporter, "I never considered the money to be mine." This was a lesson in honesty for Josh's two sons that, I believe, will stay with them for the rest of their lives.

I'll always remember this wonderful letter from a gentleman who wrote, "Several years ago, I met an individual who had reached the bottom of his ladder. Somehow, I saw in him possibilities that no one else seemed to see or even wanted to see. We became friends and, over the years, I made it possible, with encouragement and some money, for him to go back to school and get a much-desired degree. Almost finished now, and with a totally different frame of mind, he is on the way back up the ladder."

This thoughtful gentleman, I believe, will be blessed by helping this person in need. For Scripture says, "a generous person will prosper; whoever refreshes others will be refreshed" (Proverbs 11:25, NIV).

Darlene, a friend of mine who owns the music production company Trod Nossel, is always mentoring others. When I asked

> ✧ Have you aided in meeting someone else's needs in the past? Then God will always meet your needs.
>
> ✧ Have you helped to cause a special dream to come to pass for another? God will make your dreams transpire, too.
>
> ✧ Have you offered words of encouragement to a person who was down and out? In your time of distress, God will send someone to encourage you.

her why she's always willing to make someone's life a bit easier, Darlene replied, "My reward is when the recipient passes along the kindness." And by helping one another, we create a benevolent cycle. We reap what we sow. And our acts of genuine kindness and unconditional love do not go unnoticed.

Genesis 26 describes a time of great famine. Yet, in the middle of the crisis, Scripture says that, "Isaac planted crops in that land" (Genesis 26:12, NIV). Isaac didn't sit back and wait for his conditions to improve. Instead, he believed and depended on God, bringing to mind how God had previously promised to bless him (v. 3). So, Isaac, although he had never planted crops before, was industrious. As we read the rest of the passage, we find that " . . . the same year, Isaac reaped a hundredfold, because the Lord blessed him" (v. 12).

As He did with Isaac, God wants to bless you, too. The seeds you plant today can yield a grand harvest. Therefore, go out each day and be a good example. Know that God is planning great things for your future, and others will reap the benefits of your benevolent deeds for years to come.

DAY FOUR:

GAIN STRENGTH BY SERVING OTHERS.

"Blessed are the merciful, for they will be shown mercy."
MATTHEW 5:17, NIV

Mother Teresa once said:

> At the heart of silence is prayer.
> At the heart of prayer is faith.
> At the heart of faith is life.
> At the heart of life is service.

"Give and you shall receive," is one of the basic principles of life. Service to others, being kind and generous, gives our own lives meaning, purpose, and direction. And like a boomerang, that sense of happiness we get by serving others will swing right back around to us!

I recall an incredible letter I opened from a man named Rich who has been fighting cancer. In his note to me, he described that after a few years of receiving medical treatments, he was told that there was no more the doctors could do. Thereafter, his treatments were stopped.

Rich wrote, "At that point in time, when I heard the doctor say, 'There is nothing more we can do,' I simply paused to absorb his words. Then, I thanked him and his staff for all they had done and left, knowing that now I was sure God, and God alone, was my only hope."

The prognosis was grim, yet hope pushed Rich forward. This extraordinary man explained how he was not saddened: "I knew in my heart that God now had 'other concerns' He wanted to address." Tears filled my eyes as I read, and I wondered, "Other concerns?"

A humanitarian at heart, Rich, who was at this point living with a limited ability to breathe, was concerned about others. With a commitment that knows no boundaries, and carrying an oxygen bottle, he told me how he resumed his volunteer work with The United States Marine Corps, The Toys for Tots program, and The Ronald McDonald House. And after two months and three trips to the emergency room, he raised over $118,000 dollars. He explained that the money goes directly to needy children and their families. Moreover, to date, he has raised, astonishingly, over $1.9 million, all for children. Furthermore, Rich sees no end in his dedication to service; he says his passion is stronger now than it was from the first day he started.

Rich and his family were recognized with a Lifetime Achievement Award for volunteer service in addressing human needs and their dedication to the community. And then, he was personally given a Jefferson Award for service to others by the President. The Jefferson Award is given on a global basis to recognize individuals who work to make a difference in the lives of others.

Rich continued humbly in his letter, "Catherine, I was told, 'nothing more could be done for me.' But God had other plans.

With the prayers of many, loving support, and God directing my life, let me tell you what else hope and trusting in Him accomplished: Two days ago, I received a phone call that there is a new procedure that may be able to help me! If I had received the treatment they were going to perform last year, I would not be eligible for this new procedure. Now, more than ever, I believe that God has plans for my healing and plans for my future to continue my passion for helping terminal and chronically ill children. How magnificent is the God we serve."

Have you been feeling weak? Do you have any discomfort or pain? Are you nervous about your future? In studying people from every walk of life, I've discovered one main principle upon which their strength has been built: *service.* It's a simple law of living, an eternal truth that is found throughout the Bible. And when followed, it brings with it strength and abiding happiness.

✧ Deuteronomy 15:10 states, "You shall generously give to him, and your heart shall not be grieved when you give to him, because for this thing the Lord your God will bless you in all your work and in all your undertakings."

✧ Proverbs 19:17 affirms, "One who is gracious to a poor man lends to the Lord, And He will repay him for his good deed."

✧ Matthew 10:42 tells, "And whoever in the name of a disciple gives to one of these little ones even a cup of cold water to drink, truly I say to you, he shall not lose his reward."

✧ Hebrews 6:10 says, "For God is not unjust so as to forget your work and the love which you have shown toward His name, in having ministered and in still ministering to the saints" (NASB).

The more you generously give to other people, the fuller, richer, and greater your own life becomes. Give of yourself through *service* . . . and as you give out love, kindnesses, and helpfulness, the same will always come back to you.

"Some measure their lives by days and years,
Others by heart-throbs, passion, and tears;
But the surest measure under the sun,
Is what in your lifetime for others you have done."

RUTH SMELTZER

Think back on some time in your life when you were being served. How did it help you? How did you feel about those who served and assisted you? Now, here are six ideas for increasing your personal level of service:

1. Be a friend to someone and be a good listener. Venting and talking through an issue can be a huge help.
2. Do a secret act of service, such as mowing a neighbor's lawn while they are at work.
3. Donate gently used clothes, furniture, or books, or buy a couple bags of groceries and donate them to a homeless shelter.
4. Volunteer at a hospital, church, or other service organization in your community.
5. Open your home to a foster child.
6. Get involved in programs that help children, or create one of your own.

A short time ago, I read about Leland and Jan Stanford, who founded Leland Stanford Junior University. Stanford was once the governor of California, and he and his wife had a beloved son named Leland, Jr.

While on a family trip to Europe, young 15-year-old Leland passed away from typhoid fever. It has been purported that, after his son's untimely death, Stanford uttered to his wife, "The children of California shall be our children." That was the beginning of Stanford University, built as a memorial for their only child.

Devoting their energies toward making life better for others and giving of themselves in service helped the Stanfords to alleviate their own difficult circumstances, and in the process their affliction was lessened by love.

"My mother used to tell us, 'There is a destiny that makes us brothers, no one goes his way alone . . . all that we send into the lives of others, comes back, into our own.'"

TERRY MCCORMICK (A READER)

Ask yourself, "What acts of service can I carry out for someone today?" Jot down a few of them, and then carry these acts of service forth. And as you do, you will receive in greater proportion as to what you give out.

The more we scatter, the more we will reap a harvest from God's abundant bounty. And that will always be His principle.

DAY FIVE:

THE WRITTEN WORD CAN PROVIDE INSPIRATION FOR SUCCESS.

"In the beginning was the Word, and the Word was with God, and the Word was God."
JOHN 1:1, NIV

One of my favorite authors is the late Og Mandino. Although Mandino remains one of the most inspirational bestselling authors, with his books selling tens of millions and having been translated into over 25 different languages, what is most remarkable is the story of his rise to success.

In the summer of 1940, just before Mandino was to go off to college to major in journalism, his mother died suddenly, right before his eyes while she was in the kitchen fixing his lunch. Although his mother's dream for him was to be a writer, "and not just a writer—a great writer," she would remind him, he felt that, with her death, his dreams were over.

So Mandino enlisted in the Air Force, but a few years later, he returned home and moved to New York City. Buying a secondhand typewriter, he rented a small apartment and decided to try to fulfill his mother's dream. After countless attempts and presenting his writings to over 50 magazines, no one had shown any interest in his work.

When his savings were drained, he gave up on his writing aspirations. Eventually, after scores of interviews, he was hired as an insurance agent trainee, and he married.

Soon, he became addicted to drinking, and was unable to hold a job to support his young family. Finally, his wife had had enough, and she took their only child and left him. Mandino was now jobless and homeless. He drank his way across the country, doing whatever work he could find in order to survive and keep the wine flowing, and spent numerous drunken nights in gutters.

Then, one cold morning, Mandino was at the point of suicide. To stay warm, he entered a public library, and soon found himself standing in front of shelves containing scores of self-help and motivational books, and the Holy Bible. He began reading and searching, asking himself, "Where had I gone wrong? Can I make it with just a high school education? Is there any hope for me? What about my drinking problem? Is it too late for me?"

These books inspired him so much that he was determined to release the pain from the past and turn his life around. And he did.

He remarried, had a loving family, and found tremendous career success. And carrying out his mother's dream, Og Mandino became "a great writer," authoring 17 books, giving speeches all over the world, and positively influencing and motivating millions to achieve true success and happiness.

"Anyone can recede and give up; it's the easiest thing in the world to do. But to hold it together when everyone else would understand if you fell apart, that's true strength."

AUTHOR UNKNOWN

264

During a dark time in my life, a casual acquaintance gave me one of Og Mandino's books. And Og's words and his life story had a great impact on me and helped to turn my life around.

How about you? Did you ever read a book recommended by a friend that had a positive influence on your life? When was the last time you shared meaningful anecdotes, stories, and articles with other people? And what's on your list of reads this year?

For the next six months, I'd like you to read as many inspirational, wisdom, self-help, and classic books as you can. Visit your library, frequent bookstores, and search online, and select books that appeal to you. Then share what you have gleaned with someone else.

Read autobiographies of people who have overcome challenges in their lives. Afterwards, reflect on what you learned in order to assimilate the principles into your own experiences. Their prevailing stories can strongly affect you to move towards triumphing over your situation.

I know a remarkable lady who took a leap of faith and began a new endeavor that she believed would make a difference in people's lives. Having sacrificed much over the many years she spent developing her enterprise, she hit a major setback and lost almost everything that she had worked so hard to achieve. Yet, instead of wallowing in self-pity, she prayed, "God, I have done all I can. If it is your will for me to continue, you must send someone to help me."

The lady carried on and decided that she was going to be happy right where she was, enjoying her day-to-day life. Continuing her volunteer work at the hospital, she spread joy to those around her.

Then, out of the blue, the lady received a phone call from a trusted associate who said, "Yesterday, I went to lunch with an old friend. He asked about you and he wants you to call him." The next day, the lady phoned the man, who was a leading business owner in the city, and they set up a meeting.

After quietly listening to the lady's dilemma, the business owner nodded, "I will help to get your business off the ground and secure your family home." Stunned, the lady asked, "But, why?"

The man replied, "Last year, when my mother was in the hospital, you selflessly visited her and read her encouraging articles and stories."

He explained, "Those encouraging words helped my mother to heal and get well." A humble smile adorned the lady's face, as the business owner declared, "I want to bless you for the kindness you have shown my mother and countless others."

It's important to read good inspirational literature for strength. Open the Bible and read what has been penned for you by the loving hand of your Heavenly Father:

"Before I formed you in the womb I knew you . . ."
(JEREMIAH 1:5 ESV).

"I will instruct thee and teach thee in the way which thou shalt go: I will guide thee with mine eye"
(PSALM 32:8).

"[I] will rejoice over you with singing"
(ZEPHANIAH 3:17, NIV).

"[I plan] to give you hope and a future"
(JEREMIAH 29:11, NIV).

"These things I have spoken to you, that in Me you might have peace. In the world you shall have tribulation: but be of good cheer; I have overcome the world"
(JOHN 16:33, AKJV).

"Kindness is the essence of greatness and the fundamental characteristic of the noblest men and women I have known. Kindness is a passport that opens doors and fashions friends. It softens hearts and molds relationships that can last lifetimes."

JOSEPH B. WIRTHLIN

The following are some habits to adapt and share, which I believe can be helpful to gain inspiration through the written word:

✧ Host a book club: Get together with a group of friends at a regular time each week and discuss a certain book.

✧ Consider starting a blog and writing about books you've read and enjoyed.

✧ Make copies of uplifting articles or poems and mail them to those who need a boost.

✧ Write positive statements, Biblical principles, and inspirational quotes on index cards and read them each day.

✧ Wear jewelry, accessories, or articles of clothing that contain a special message, such as a "Life is good" shirt, a cross necklace with the word "believe" in the center, a silver cuff bracelet with "This too shall pass" engraved on the cuff, or a purse with a Scripture verse inside.

A reader from Michigan stated, "God's Word and your book have been helping me through a tough time the last two months.

My company had a financial downfall and laid us off before Christmas. I pray every day and know that God has a great and wonderful plan for my life and I am expecting a great new job any day now.

"Through all of this, God has shown me more blessings than I would have ever thought of or imagined. The time alone with Him has been wonderful, but sometimes silent. Then, the blessings show up! How amazing is our God!"

And, as day follows night, miracles will follow you.

Kitty, who is retiring from the teaching profession after 38 years, collects e-mail forwards that contain positive thoughts. She cuts them out and pastes them in a scrapbook. When she feels the need to be uplifted, she takes out the book and reads it over. Kitty says this helps her focus on the positive. Tip: Make a "positive thoughts" scrapbook, as well, filled with mementoes, cards, and photographs to review and keep your thoughts going in a good direction.

DAY SIX:

TAKE GOD'S HAND AND HE WILL LEAD YOU TO VICTORY.

"I lift up my eyes to the mountains—where does my help come from? My help comes from the Lord, the Maker of heaven and earth. He will not let your foot slip—he who watches over you will not slumber; indeed, He who watches over Israel will neither slumber nor sleep. The Lord watches over you—the Lord is your shade at your right hand; the sun will not harm you by day, nor the moon by night. The Lord will keep you from all harm—he will watch over your life; the Lord will watch over your coming and going both now and forevermore."

PSALM 121:1-8, NIV

Are you going through difficulties? Remember, the two key words here are "going through." Maybe you are undergoing a challenging circumstance, experiencing an unforeseen problem, or are being treated unfairly. And perhaps you are asking yourself, "How can I achieve my dreams now?" Maybe you are then declaring, "I'll never overcome that obstacle," "I don't have the ability," or "I have waited so long already." Yet, be careful not to fall into despair. If you mull over the problem, and keep wondering "why me?" and constantly talking negatively about it, you will magnify the difficulty, rather than magnifying God.

You will go through adversity; nevertheless, your time of trouble shall pass. The tide will change, and you will prevail over tough situations. Bear in mind, God is greater than the mountains you are climbing, the burdens you're carrying, or the giants you have faced.

Therefore, get to know God, for the more you know Him, the more you will trust Him. Here are four ways to do so:

1. Since the Bible is God's Word, I suggest that you read from it every day to grow spiritually. In the morning, for ten minutes, underline faith-building, victorious verses in your Bible. This will provide you with strength and wisdom regarding the outcome of any dilemma and help you to gain victory over your situation.

   Here are a few victorious verses to highlight:

❖ "We are more than a conqueror through Him who loved us." ROMANS 8:37, ESV

❖ "For the Lord your God is the one who goes with you to fight for you against your enemies to give you victory." DEUTERONOMY 20:4, NIV

❖ "Do not be overcome by evil, but overcome evil with good." ROMANS 12:21, NIV

❖ "The Lord is faithful, and He will strengthen and protect you." 2 THESSALONIANS 3:3, NIV

❖ "The Lord your God is with you, He is mighty to save. He will take great delight in you, He will quiet you with his love, He will rejoice over you with singing." ZEPHANIAH 3:17, NIV

2. Thereafter, memorize a verse a week. Read it out loud a few times and use vivid images to help you memorize the Scripture

faster. You can also try writing the Scripture on a message board at home or at work, taping an index card with the Scripture on it to your car dashboard, or keeping it programmed into your phone for the week.

3. Then, pray daily, and especially before bedtime, for God wants to hear from you, and prayer is vital to your spiritual growth. Jesus states: "If ye shall say unto this mountain, be thou removed, and be thou cast into the sea; it shall be done. And all things whatsoever ye shall ask in prayer, believing, ye shall receive" (Matthew 21:21-22). Not only does God promise to answer your prayers, but as you pray, He will also provide guidance.

4. Next, share with others real-life testimonies that you have experienced. The Bible says that, "Whoever acknowledges me before men, I will also acknowledge him before my Father in heaven" (Matthew 10:32).

A letter was mailed to me from a gentleman I'll call Dan. He wrote and described how every statistic was stacked up against him: he grew up in a dysfunctional home, lived in poverty, was ostracized as a child, and encountered many destructive experiences over the course of his young life. And when he listened to those who would tell him that he "didn't have a future," his attitude really began to deteriorate.

Yet, with prayer and the strong faith that he had learned from his grandmother, plus sheer determination, Dan strongly believed he would overcome the negativity of his past. Dan knew the Scriptures, because throughout his childhood, his grandmother would read him strength-giving passages. Dan had those passages in his memory bank and, with God's word giving him strength, he decided to let go of the old wounds inflicted on him by others and, instead, look toward his future dreams.

During high school, Dan got a job at a restaurant cleaning tables. Then, he worked his way up the ladder, from cleaning tables, to ordering the supplies, and after that waiting on the customers. The owner of the restaurant saw the eagerness, strong work ethic, and tenacity of this young man and he encouraged him to attend a local college. Dan followed his advice and the restaurant owner became his mentor. He taught Dan all aspects of the business, and Dan excelled. Years later, when it came time for the owner to retire, Dan heartily took over the establishment.

Today, Dan is a successful restaurant owner, generous to noble causes, and well respected in the community, as he shares is strength and knowledge to help others get ahead. He's married, with a happy home life, and two loving children. Dan wrote, "Regardless of how many failures you encounter, if you trust God, read His word, and don't give up, success is still attainable."

In Acts chapter 3, Peter and John were going to the temple for a time of prayer. A man who had been crippled since birth was regularly carried to the temple's gate, where he would solicit donations on his own behalf from the generosity of others.

As Peter was about to go into the temple, he fastened his eyes on the lame man. Peter then asked the man to look upon him and John, and he did. "So the man gave them his attention, expecting to get something from them" (Acts 3:5 NIV).

Then, Peter said, "Silver or gold I do not have, but what I do have I give you. In the name of Jesus Christ of Nazareth, walk" (v. 6). Although Peter didn't have any money, Luke 9:1-6 tells us that he had the power and authority from Jesus to "drive out all demons and to cure diseases" (v. 1).

Boldly, Peter took the man by his right hand and lifted him up. Instantly, the man's feet and ankles became strong, and he jumped to his feet and began to walk. This man had expected something in faith—a small donation—but he was given abundantly more, for now he was healed. And all he could do in response was praise and worship God. Thereafter, the man walked into the temple with the apostles, and the people who were gathered saw his miraculous transformation and were filled with wonder and amazement. God's hand, indeed, had led him to victory.

Each day do the best you can with what you have been given. Prepare yourself for success. For the day will come when God opens the window and you will need to be ready to go through it. In a moment, you can go from seeming failure to great success, from sickness to complete health, from shortage to abundance.

In the evening, before I go to sleep, my fluffy orange cat named Chris snuggles right beside me. If I turn to my left side, he turns. If I turn round to my right, Chris turns. The cat wants his little face directly next to mine. In the same way, we must turn our face toward God, reading His word and looking to Him for help.

God is grooming you for special work and is leading you to greater blessings and achievements. No matter where you are, who you are, or what has happened in the past, take God's hand, read His word, and one day, you will stand in wonder to see what a stunning victory He has made of your life.

Remember to, as David wrote in the Psalms, "Seek His face always" (105:4, NIV), for God's face is continually turned lovingly toward you.

DAY SEVEN:

THE WILL TO EXCEL CONQUERS OBSTACLES.

"Be glad for all God is planning for you . . . "

ROMANS 12:12, NLT

Famed football coach Vince Lombardi once said, "The spirit, the will to win, and the will to excel are the things that endure. These qualities are so much more important than the events that occur."

On the road of life, there are struggles and stumbling blocks all along the way. We experience disappointments and setbacks, and hurdles that sometimes seem insurmountable. For daily living is full of evolving challenges: a delay here, an uneasy feeling there, an adverse situation that must be overcome. And because of the myriad of trials we face, we sometimes have doubts that the dreams of our heart, which one by one have been pushed aside, can still come to pass.

But obstacles don't have to stop you. Focus on what's important to you and commit to that vision. Do the very best you can, take one step at a time—and you will reach your destination.

Suggestion: Have a plan "B" and a plan "C." Backup plans
will put you in a position of strength.

I like what Nobel Prize winner Nelson Mandela declared, "The
greatest glory in living lies not in never falling, but in rising every
time we fall." So, if you have been knocked down, let me help
you back up again. There's so much further for you to go. There
are still great possibilities ahead of you. You have the God-given
resolve and the fortitude to succeed. For the difference between
what is "possible" and what's "impossible" to achieve, I believe,
lies in your steadfast determination.

In retrospect, I recognize why God has allowed certain
events to transpire in my own life. I've found that often, God
gives us certain tests to prepare us for what's to come. Read
Genesis 6:5-22 and you will discover the test that God gave
Noah, summarized here:

"God saw how corrupt the earth had become, for all the people
on earth had corrupted their ways" (v. 12). He decided to wipe
away mankind, "but Noah found favor in the eyes of the Lord" (v.
8). With very specific instructions, God commanded Noah to build
a huge ark for him and his family, and they were to take with them
animals and creatures of all kinds, in preparation for a flood that
would destroy every living thing on earth. Noah was a righteous
man and, with a strong will, obeyed God. He "did everything just
as God commanded him" (v. 22). As a result, Noah's resolve has
been an example for us to follow through all time.

Here are some questions to think about: Consider the incidents
you have encountered this past year—what did you learn about

yourself or others? Did these occurrences help you grow? Were you able to pass on that wisdom and knowledge to others?

What about the events that have transpired over your lifetime— what have you discovered about yourself? Have you uncovered newfound strengths? Do you now have the gift of understanding, a more compassionate heart, or a more generous spirit? What lessons have you learned that can be the springboard to future success? What other ways have those experiences helped to shape the person who you currently are? Does your life set an example?

Compose a list of a half-dozen past experiences that helped you to become who you are today. Each experience we encounter can be an instrument that God uses to form us to become the people He intended for us to be.

When I was in grade school, I was in an oratory contest. To this day, I still recall how nervous I was speaking onstage, in front of the entire school. My hands shook, my voice cracked, and my face must have turned four shades of red, as I attempted to recite my speech. Though, now, I am not frightened at all to speak in front of an audience, or live on national television in front of millions of people. Why? Because I already went through the nervousness of public speaking, and hence, I am not afraid anymore.

Likewise, you may need to develop in a certain area before you can take on that new task or endeavor that's been on your mind. You might have to learn how to deal with people with different insights, so you can grow in your career. Or, perhaps, you must gain more real-life experiences, in order to have a greater impact when helping others. Regardless of how difficult your current situation may be it could be the preparation you require for the ultimate design God has for you.

"Always bear in mind that your own resolution to succeed is more important than any other one thing."

ABRAHAM LINCOLN

Years ago, a friend of mine was in a terrible relationship. After she finally broke it off with her boyfriend, with great determination she finished her education and became a nurse. With the hard lessons she had learned from her previous relationship, she knew what she wanted in a life partner, and even jotted down on a piece of paper a list of attributes she hoped to one day find in a husband.

Time passed, and my friend held onto the dream in her heart of someday being married to her soul mate. She continued to enjoy her life, traveling, participating in hobbies, and advancing her career. Some would shake their heads and say disapprovingly to her, "You're getting older," and "Your biological clock is ticking." One person even uttered, "Stop being so fussy, there must be someone suitable for you to settle down with and marry!"

Those negative words hurt. However, my friend mustered the strength to ignore the remarks and was unwavering as she plodded onward. "I paid no attention to the hurtful comments and insults," she declared. "I didn't get caught up in defending myself and I avoided arguments. It doesn't bring any benefit and just wastes time and energy."

My friend told me how she didn't want to just "settle" for "less than" the perfect mate God had for her. She asked the

Lord to give her strength to see her heart's dream come true, and thus, she remained patient, even though her prayers were not yet answered. For silence does not mean God is idle. Remember, it takes careful arranging and precise planning for God to line up the right people and right circumstances that are best for us.

Then, at the hospital, quite unexpectedly, one thing led to another and my friend met a wonderful man who was an employee there. They began dating. Six months later, they joyfully got engaged and a year later, were married. Now, they share a wonderful life together with their precious little girl, and my friend is now expecting their second child.

I want you to remind yourself that adversity is not permanent. On the other side of the trial, there is joy in abundance. And, in time, you may see the purpose behind the difficulty. Our circumstances may not immediately change. Yet, God can change us to meet our circumstances. Think about the apostle Paul. He was thrown into a dungeon, all the while writing words that would encourage us for a lifetime.

Awhile ago, I received an unforgettable letter from a man who, after 11 years, was being released from prison. On a sheet of plain white, lined paper, he wrote to tell me that week after week, year after year, his mother would send him copies of my weekly newspaper column, and that he has been blessed by them. Everything that happened previously in his life had worked together to bring him to this defining moment of his release from prison. At the close of his letter, he wrote, "Catherine, I am finally going home a new person."

"I've missed more than 9,000 shots in my career.
I've lost almost 300 games. Twenty-six times,
I've been trusted to take the game-winning shot,

and missed. I've failed over and over and over again in my life. And that is why I succeed."

MICHAEL JORDAN

So, when life throws you a curveball, with a strong will and a determined spirit, move beyond your past setbacks and see them as stepping-stones to success. And when all is said and done, you will have the victory!

WINDOW EIGHT

GIVE THANKS FOR GOD'S BLESSINGS

"If anyone would tell you the shortest, surest way to all happiness, and all perfection, he must tell you to make it a rule to yourself to thank and praise God for everything that happens to you. For it is certain that whatever seeming calamity happens to you, if you thank and praise God for it, you turn it into a blessing."

WILLIAM LAW, EIGHTEENTH-CENTURY MINISTER

DAY ONE:

GIVE THANKS DAILY AND YOUR SPIRITS WILL SOAR.

"Oh, give thanks to the Lord, for He is good!
For His mercy endures forever."
1 CHRONICLES 16:34, NKJV

There was once a tale told about an enemy who wanted to plant his seeds of discouragement into the hearts of men and women everywhere. However, there was one place where the seeds could not take root and grow.

On a Saturday morning, the enemy was asked by one of his curious followers, "Where is the one place where those seeds of discouragement wouldn't thrive?" At first the enemy didn't answer. You could have heard a pin drop. Eventually, the enemy replied, "Seeds of discouragement cannot grow in the heart of a habitually thankful person."

How thankful are you? Are you grateful at all times, or only when things are going well?

Maybe you have accumulated so many disappointments over the years that you wonder, "How can I be thankful when the trials of life seem to overwhelm me?" Well, that is especially the time to give thanks, for thankfulness is a powerful tool that can lift you out of despair and make your spirit soar. Thankfulness can instantly change your attitude about yourself and your conditions.

"Gratitude can transform common days into thanksgivings, turn routine jobs into joy, and change ordinary opportunities into blessings."

William Arthur Ward

In three easy steps, here is a method for how you can look on the "bright side" of common, everyday situations.

✧ First: Identify something that makes you upset, such as, being stuck in traffic on your way home from work.

✧ Second: Declare some affirmative statements about the circumstance. For instance: Say, "Yes, I am in traffic, but I'm grateful I am healthy enough to drive," "I'm thankful to have a car," or "I am happy that I am employed."

✧ Third: Ponder on the positives and all you have for which to be grateful.

I received an interesting e-mail from Tom, a gentleman from the Midwest who wrote about the importance of thankfulness. "When I used to hear people talk about the great importance of being thankful all the time, and in all circumstances, I used to be very skeptical. But I kept noticing that the happiest people were constantly expressing thankfulness and appreciation for the people and things in their lives. So, I took a chance and tried it."

Tom's letter continued, "I just made a decision to be thankful every day, several times a day, for whatever people and things [were] in my life. And I noticed that it did bring me happiness. I expressed thanks for my car, my computer, my apartment, my shoes, my teeth, my eyes, my hands, my feet, my health, and so on. Then, something good happened—I started feeling much better every day! Moreover, I saw that God will smooth the path to our achieving what we currently don't have if we *appreciate what we already do have*. Now I see that thankfulness is the miraculous path to happiness for today and tomorrow and all our tomorrows."

Mother Teresa said, "There is more hunger for love and appreciation in this world than for bread." Therefore, daily, smile, radiate joy, and convey love and appreciation to those around you. Make it a point to offer a few flattering remarks to others each day. And don't forget your furry friends; pet your dog, kiss your puppy on the head, snuggle with a cat on the couch, and tell them you love them! Everyone, even your pets, likes to know that they're appreciated. Their positive reactions can help to put you in a great mood, too.

As with Tom, we must be thankful and look for the best in all circumstances, taking the time to thank God, bringing to mind His love and faithfulness. Let's appreciate and focus on all that is right in our lives. Gratitude enlarges the heart, and allows even more goodness to enter it, thus helping us to create the future we desire.

> *"What if you gave someone a gift, and they neglected to thank you for it—would you be likely to give them another? Life is the same way. In order to attract more of the blessings that life has to offer, you must truly appreciate what you already have."*
>
> RALPH MARSTON

What you put your attention on expands in your life. So to get yourself into a place of reflection and gratitude, I suggest that you create a "Gratitude Journal." Keep a notepad and pen on your nightstand and, before bedtime, and on a regular basis at other times in the day, record two or three things for which you are grateful. Write about whatever was good and right for that particular day. Then, thank God for each blessing. After a while, you will tend to notice special things that enhance your life and give you joy. And you'll begin to include in your Gratitude Journal things that, perhaps, you wouldn't have otherwise noticed. Here's a great tip: Whenever you are feeling anxious or upset, read over your journal for a great pick-me-up.

> *"Nothing is more honorable than a grateful heart."*
>
> SENECA

About a month ago, my daughter Lauren and I had to take our tabby cat, Mickey, to the veterinarian's office for a check-up. We got into the car, and I slowly drove up the steep hill away from our home, so as not to disturb our meowing cat in the kitty carrying case that we had placed in the backseat. As I gingerly approached the stop sign at the top of the hill, suddenly a blue car came flying across the road and hit the tree just twenty feet in front of my car.

Thankfully, the young man in the car was not hurt, and he was actually able to jump out of the smashed car through his driver side window. Now, if I had not been driving so slowly because I did not want to frighten our cat, that car would have hit us head-on. Lauren and I both uttered prayers of thankfulness to God for His hand of protection and the gift of another day.

Life is fragile. That must be why Scripture tells us in Psalm 90:12 to "Teach us to number our days aright, that we may gain a heart of wisdom" (NIV). Every moment that we live is a treasure, each breath a gift, so let's not take it for granted.

When we read chapter 3 of the Book of Habakkuk in the Old Testament, we learn that most of what the prophet Habakkuk wrote about was miraculous acts of God from the past. Habakkuk was looking back in reverence to the great things God had done: when he rescued His people from Egypt; the way in which He overcame the Egyptians and parted the Red Sea; and how, at the request of Joshua, "The sun and moon stood still in their habitation" (3:11).

Why was Habakkuk looking back at yesterday? Because he was living in difficult, unjust times and wanted to remember what the majesty of God had done before, to give him encouragement, strength, and hope for the future. Habakkuk knew that God was capable of doing all things. So, even as he viewed the outward circumstances of his present, adverse afflictions, he knew all was not lost, for he believed God could intervene and bring him through triumphantly. Habakkuk resolved to be joyful and rejoice in the Lord, as we see in the song of worship he wrote: "Though the fig tree does not bud and there are no grapes on the vines, though the olive crop fails and the fields produce no food, though there are no sheep in the pen and no cattle in the stalls, yet I will rejoice in the Lord, I will be joyful in God my Savior" (Habakkuk 3:17-18, NIV).

In spite of it all, no matter how bleak the probability of success appears is in whatever we face, or when life just doesn't make sense, we must always keep God in the forefront of our minds, and like Habakkuk, in our hearts rejoice in the Lord.

Look around you today. Think about your blessings, past and present, write about them, and verbalize your thanks and appreciation to God and others. Don't ever get tired of thanking God for His goodness. And tell other people what God has done: the miracles, the favor, His protection. For, as you do, God will bestow His blessings in even greater portions.

P.S. I appreciate and love you!

DAY TWO:

EVERY THORN IN LIFE HAS A PURPOSE, SO REMAIN THANKFUL.

"Give thanks in all circumstances."
1 THESSALONIANS 5:18, NIV

One morning before school, my daughter was finishing her breakfast and asked, "Mom, can I bring some roses in to my teacher?" Pouring her a glass of milk, I replied, "Sure, honey. I'll make a bouquet for you." I grabbed a pair of scissors and scurried out the door.

The crisp air was refreshing as I stepped outside. Then, I turned and I saw the rose bushes on the side of our home ablaze with magenta. I reached into the center of the abundant plant, but in a rush to snip the roses off the bush for my daughter before the bus came, I scratched and cut my arm on the thorns.

When I walked back inside and my sensitive daughter saw the blood running down my arm, she almost started crying. "I'm okay, don't worry," I consoled her, and I reached for a washcloth to wipe the blood away.

Her whimpers subsided and she perceptively inquired,

"Mom, it's not fair. . . . Why does God allow thorns?" I pondered my daughter's question for a minute, knowing that this was an opportunity to explain to her an important life lesson. Hence, I took a deep breath, and responded, "Honey, just as we are thankful to God for the beautiful roses, we should also thank Him for the thorns."

Wide-eyed, she exclaimed, "What? Be thankful for thorns!" The perplexed look on my daughter's face told me she didn't understand my statement.

And so, I continued, "Even when we don't understand *why* or *what's happening* with our situation, know that God will use it for our greater good."

I leaned closer to her, "God never sends us out alone, whether we are in the middle of a patch of thorns or a bed of roses, He is with us. Let's continue to thank Him."

> *"Reflect upon your present blessings, of which every man has plenty; not on your past misfortunes, of which all men have some."*
>
> CHARLES DICKENS

Yet, sometimes, it's hard to remain thankful, for in many ways, on many fronts, life is full of ongoing challenges. And through the suffering we face, it is easy to get embittered and fall back, despairing.

But if you are feeling down or filled with stress because of "the thorns of life," today I will guide you through a technique that I do, which helps me to unclutter my mind, shift my mood, refocus, and reflect on thankfulness. It's called "The Thankful Walk."

1. Preferably in the sunlight, take a walk in nature and with each step think about thankfulness. Try walking for 45 minutes or longer along the beach, through a park, in the center of your town, in your neighborhood, or around an outdoor track.

2. Carry in your pocket a mini tape recorder or a small notepad and pencil.

3. As you walk, breathe in, exhale slowly, and experience the awe and wonder of the natural world. Pay attention to the things coming in through your God-given senses—the birds singing, the smell of the flowers, the sound of children's laughter, and see how many things you can find for which to be thankful.

4. Make notes, via your tape recorder or notepad, of all the answers and creative thoughts that come into your mind with each step, and thank God for them. I get some of my best ideas this way!

When you return home, list everything you discovered on your thankful walk. You should feel calmer and more peaceful, for a cardiovascular exercise such as walking helps to ward off anxiety by releasing the body's natural "feel-good" chemicals. Thus, you should come home with a positive boost in your mood and a better perspective on the "thorns" you may be tackling.

> *"He is a wise man who does not grieve for the things which he has not, but rejoices for those which he has."*
>
> EPICTETUS

God often leads us through tough times to demonstrate His tremendous power, helping us to learn to rely upon Him, drawing us to His glorious presence. Moreover, although "the thorns of life" don't always make immediate sense, we should not let them ruin our entire outlook, allowing us to become negative or resentful. "You do not realize now what I am doing, but later you will understand," assures Jesus in John 13:7 (NIV). In the Old Testament, 2 Kings 4:1-7, we learn about The Widow's Oil.

The story began tragically. A woman's husband died and

he left her in severe financial ruin. She had no money and was faced with disaster. To make matters worse, the creditors were demanding payment and threatening to take her two sons as slaves in compensation for her husband's debt.

Yet, the widow had great faith in God. She needed a miracle and believed God would help her, so she cried out to Elisha, who was God's prophet, and told him her desperate plight.

"Elisha replied to her, 'How can I help you? Tell me, what do you have in your house?' And she said, 'Your woman servant has nothing there at all,' she said, 'except a small jar of olive oil'" (v. 2, NIV).

So, Elisha asked her to do something unusual. "Elisha said, 'Go around and ask all your neighbors for empty jars. Don't ask for just a few. Then go inside and shut the door behind you and your sons. Pour oil into all the jars, and as each is filled, put it to one side'" (v. 3-4, NIV).

The widow didn't know why she was being asked to go from door to door asking her neighbors to borrow empty jars. But, in obedience to God, she followed Elisha's directions.

Thereafter, her sons brought all the jars to her that they had collected. She took out her small jar of oil and she began to pour. One, two, three, jar after jar, the widow kept on pouring the olive oil into each container. Miraculously, it continued flowing, and she had enough oil to fill each jar.

Elisha then informed the widow that she could sell the olive oil to solve her financial difficulties, and there would be enough money left over for her and her sons to live on. God had given her more than the bare necessities. And the widow was thankful to God that He had poured out His grace and provision into their lives.

"God is in charge," writes a reader from Mississippi. "And the more we thank Him, the more God gives us the strength to carry on, and in His extraordinary timing, our seeming difficulty will deliver unexpected gifts."

When I picked my daughter up that day from school, as

Write a letter to God. In the letter, pour out your thoughts and tell Him everything for which you are thankful.

soon as she got into the car, she recounted how she had given the bouquet of pink roses to her teacher. Subsequently, she dug into her backpack and handed me a note. It read: "Thank you for the beautiful bouquet. My husband has been ill and he just had surgery. I was praying to God that everything would be all right, and those roses came at just the right moment. They were a symbol of hope and the encouragement that I needed to get through this trauma."

I folded the notecard, looked at the deep scratches on my arm, and thought to myself, "Every thorn we encounter does have a purpose." And I recalled that the Bible says, "Blessed be God . . . who comforteth us in all our tribulation that we may be able to comfort them which are in any trouble, by the comfort wherewith we ourselves are comforted by God" (2 Corinthians 1:3-4).

"If you concentrate on finding whatever is good in every situation, you will discover that your life will suddenly be filled with gratitude, a feeling that nurtures the soul."

RABBI HAROLD KUSHNER

This week, I'd like you to slow down, and begin the daily ritual of taking at least five minutes each morning to privately give thanks to God. Notice all the blessings in your life. And with a heart of gratitude, keep rejoicing in Him, being thankful for the roses and the thorns. Then, keep an eye out for what God will do next. Get ready—He loves to astound us with His goodness!

DAY THREE:

TAKE RESIDENCE ON HAPPY VALLEY ROAD.

*"Both riches and honor come from You, and You reign over all.
In Your hands are power and might; in Your hands it is to make
great and to give strength to all. Now therefore, our God, we
thank You and praise Your glorious name."*
1 CHRONICLES 29:12-13, AMP

Years back, I read a wonderful piece of writing by author Napoleon
Hill:

"The richest man in the world lives in Happy Valley. He is
rich in values that endure, in things he cannot lose. Here is an
inventory of his riches and how he acquired them:

I found happiness by helping others find it.

*I found sound health by living temperately and eating only
the food my body requires to maintain itself.*

I hate no man, envy no man, but love and respect all mankind.

*I am engaged in a labor of love with which I mix play
generously; therefore, I seldom grow tired.*

I pray daily, not for more riches, but for more wisdom with which to recognize, embrace, and enjoy the great abundance of riches I already possess.

I speak no name save only to honor it, and I slander no man for any cause whatsoever.

I ask no favors of anyone except the privilege of sharing my blessings with all who desire them.

I am on good terms with my conscience; therefore, it guides me accurately in everything I do.

I have more material wealth than I need because I am free from greed and covet only those things I can use constructively while I live.

My wealth comes from those whom I have benefited by sharing my blessings.

The estate of happy valley, which I own, is not taxable. It exists mainly in my own mind, in intangible riches that cannot be assessed for taxation and appropriated except by those who adopt my way of life. I created this estate over a lifetime of effort by observing nature's laws and forming habits to conform with them."

Many people associate happiness with an external pursuit. Yet, happiness is already within you and within your reach. Today, I would like you to sit down with a cup of coffee or tea and ask yourself some questions such as: "What thoughts am I allowing myself to think? How can I control my own thinking? Am I making a conscious effort to think optimistically?" Make note of your answers.

Your thoughts are similar to a magnet and can attract to you the things that you desire. Happiness is first fashioned in the mind. And your mind belongs to you. Hence, you can influence

> *"I am determined to be cheerful and happy, in whatever situation I may be; for I have also learned from experience that the greater part of our happiness or misery depends upon our dispositions, and not upon our circumstances."*
>
> MARTHA WASHINGTON

the quality of your life by the thoughts you allow therein.

King Solomon had "a wise and discerning heart," given to him by the Lord (1 Kings 3:12, NIV). God's favor was with him, as Solomon built the marvelous Temple. He was also blessed with wealth, power, and privilege. Yet, as time went on, King Solomon's great resources, accumulated knowledge, and pursuits did not bring him lasting happiness.

His attitude became one of self-indulgence; he encouraged idolatry, and he chose to surround himself with immorality and corrupt worldly pleasures. Solomon turned his heart away from the Lord, mishandled God's gifts, and was led astray. Materially, King Solomon had everything he needed to enjoy life, but he found that it was insignificant, for he had discovered that life was empty, apart from God.

In conclusion, King Solomon came to understand that God should be at the center of all we undertake, that true happiness, peace, and thanksgiving come when we have the attitude that loves and obeys God, as we align ourselves with His will. In Ecclesiastes 12:13 (NIV), Solomon wrote, "Fear God and keep His commandments; for this is the duty of all mankind." King Solomon even ended up authoring three books of the Bible: most of the Proverbs, Ecclesiastes, and the Song of Solomon.

Daily, try this ritual to bring more peace and happiness into your life: Repeat often phrases such as: "I'm grateful to God to be alive and well." "I'm appreciative for my healthy mind and body." "I'm thankful for our country." "I'm indebted to our servicemen and servicewomen." "I am pleased that I can share my gifts with the world." "I am glad for all the people in my life." "I'm at peace with others." "I am grateful for the food I have to eat." "I am thankful for my home." Now, think of a dozen more reasons to be happy and give thanks. Recite them and put them into your memory bank. Just as an athlete consistently trains his or her body, if you have seen the glass as "half empty" in the past, with this exercise, you can retrain your mind to see the glass as "half full."

Each day, I'd like you to do something nice for yourself. For instance, put on some relaxing music, go to the library and read a few pages of an inspirational book, read the Ten Commandments or an encouraging Bible story, eat some delicious dark chocolate and flip through a decorating magazine, go fishing, try a yoga class, or take a stroll with your dog while listening to a motivational CD or podcast. Notice how your mindset has changed after the enjoyable activity.

Last August, I developed a condition called frozen shoulder. Temporarily, my right arm lost its range of motion. The doctor suggested that, until my condition improved, I should learn to do everything on my left side.

Being right-handed, I thought, "I'm not sure that I can only use my left side," and confessed that sentiment to the doctor. "Sure, you'll be able to," the doctor encouraged, "if you are willing to practice."

The same principle holds true for reprogramming our own dominant thought pattern from negative to positive. Like learning to use my left arm, it's just a matter of effort and practice!

> *"Whether you think you can or whether you think you can't—you're right."*
>
> HENRY FORD

At our home, we have four beautiful cats: Mickey, Chris, Sam, and Grace. And whenever our littlest kitty, Grace, hears the can opener turning, she runs into the kitchen. It doesn't matter what time of the day or night it is, or whether she is sleeping or awake, when Grace hears that noise, she thinks it's her food and she scampers in that direction.

Just as Grace dashes at the sound of the can opener, you can discipline yourself to run toward the positives.

1. Recognize God's goodness in your day-to-day life. And recall the miracles that God has done for you previously.
2. Participate in activities that you love, spend time outdoors, and exercise. Your outlook will always be brighter after a fitness class, bike ride, or brisk walk.
3. Find good humor in situations and focus on solutions, not problems.
4. Associate with happy people, for happiness is contagious.

> *"Great hearts send forth steadily the secret forces that incessantly draw great events, and wherever the mind of man goes, nature will accompany him, no matter what the path."*
>
> RALPH WALDO EMERSON

298

Despite what has transpired in the past, never be critical toward yourself, dwelling on mistakes, guilt, or feelings of inadequacy, thinking you can't do anything right. If a negative notion comes into your mind, immediately substitute it with a constructive statement. Several times a day, affirm with confidence, "I'm happy," "I am opening the window of my heart to a new beginning," and "There is so much in my world God has given to me for which to be thankful."

You have everything you need to begin to harness the strength of your mind. God is planning to do great things in your future. So show your love to God, align yourself to His perfect will, see the possibilities around you, and look forward in joyful anticipation to what's to come. Be good to people and put God at the center of everything you undertake. Smile often, and act and speak in a positive way, and your attitude will respond to these choices.

Happiness is there . . . and it's waiting for you!

DAY FOUR:

REJOICE AND PRAISE GOD IN ADVANCE, AND FIND REST.

"We sought Him and He has given us rest on every side."

2 CHRONICLES 14:7, NIV

Long ago, I read a story about a woman who was upset because of the heavy cross that she carried. When she looked at her friends and neighbors, she wished that she could change places with them and carry their cross instead. "Surely their cross would be lighter than mine," she thought to herself.

That night the woman had a dream, and in her dream she was in a grand room surrounded by crosses of various shapes and sizes. The room was filled to capacity with crosses both large and small. As the woman looked to the left, there was an exquisite cross that was covered with jewels. It was lovely, so she walked over to it. "I want that cross," she uttered, trying to pick it up. But the weight of that cross was too heavy for her to bear.

Her gaze fell on another cross. This one was superb, intertwined with large, bright flowers around its base. However, when the woman tried to lift it, the rugged edges scratched her skin.

She took a deep breath and began to become disheartened. Just then, she turned and saw a simple, plain cross. As she moved closer to it, she lifted it easily. Next, with a sense of familiarity, she declared, "This is my old comfortable cross." Contented that she had found it, she soon realized that it was the lightest of all of the crosses, and she began to praise God, and found that with God's help, she was able to carry it.

Do you have a challenge to overcome? Are you struggling with a situation and you just don't know what to do next? Is your patience pushed to the limit? Instead of wallowing in doubts and anxiety, take some time to humbly praise God. There is wondrous power in praise.

1. God can give us hope, where there seems to be hopelessness.
2. He can provide direction when we're temporarily lost.
3. And He offers encouragement when we are oppressed.

> *"God gave you a gift of 86,400 seconds*
> *today. Have you used one to say 'thank you'?"*
>
> WILLIAM A. WARD

Exhale worries and cares and inhale love and thankfulness, remembering that God is greater than any problem you might face. Think about it this way: He has guided you thus far and He will continue to guide you. Recall Acts 16, when Paul and Silas were thrown into prison. They were locked up, their feet were fastened, and they were confined to a cell. Paul and Silas's circumstances were grim and their future appeared to be hopeless. However, with boldness and confidence they kept their focus on trusting in and praising God.

Verses 25-26 say, "About midnight Paul and Silas were praying and singing hymns to God, and the other prisoners were listening to them. Suddenly there was such a violent earthquake that the foundations of the prison were shaken. At once, all the prison doors flew open, and everybody's chains came loose."

One moment, things looked bleak. Yet swiftly, in the next instant, God moved and the chains that were holding Paul and Silas back were broken off of them and the prison walls came tumbling down. The power of God altered the situation.

Maybe a door has closed behind you and you're unsure about the future. Perhaps, you feel confined in the chains of the past. Or you may be bound by shackles of worry and you think there is no reason to count your blessings or to praise God. But if you "rejoice evermore" (1 Thessalonians 5:16), lifting your voice in praise and thanksgiving, God will hear you and He will help you. And soon, similar to Paul and Silas, you will experience a tremendous breakthrough.

> *"Thou that has given so much to me,*
> *Give one thing more, a grateful heart;*
> *Not thankful, when it pleaseth me,*
> *As if thy blessings had spare days;*
> *But such a heart, whose pulse may be*
> *Thy praise."*
> GEORGE HERBERT

I'd like you to think of something right now that you want God to do for you. Once you have your specific heart's desire fixed in your mind, praise Him "as though it is already done." Believe it. And prepare for the desire to come to pass. Rest assured, God will respond to your action and praise.

The key is not to complain about what is in front of our eyes "at this instant," but to rejoice and thank God "in advance" for what is to come in the near future.

✧ If you are out of work, don't sit back and say, "I'll never find another job." In place of this, say, "Thank you, God, for the ideal career you have set up for me."

✧ If you are searching for a new relationship, do not walk around with your head down and think, "I'm running out of time," or "I could grow old bitter and alone." Instead, say to God, "I praise you for bringing the perfect person into my life."

✧ If you or a loved one is sick, never give up and state, "There is no hope for recovery." Rather, declare with faith, "God, you are strong and mighty and I trust that you have the complete ability and authority to restore my (or my loved one's) health."

Try this creative project: God deserves praise. If you're a good poet or writer, or are musically inclined, compose your own poems or songs that praise and glorify God's greatness and tell Him how thankful you are for all that He bestows. Who knows, you may have a musical hit or the next bestseller!

A few months ago, a friend of mine's husband was admitted into the hospital for a serious surgical procedure. Sometime later, when I visited her at their home, I asked, "How did you handle that stressful time?" She said that when she was sitting in the hospital waiting room, instead of being overwhelmed by her husband's condition, she distracted herself by taking out a pen and paper from her purse and making a list of the blessings in her life, and she praised God over and over for making her husband well.

"In fact," my friend told me, as she arranged the carnations I had brought to her into a vase, "what was amazing was the more I praised God and re-read my thankful list, the more reassured and contented I became . . . even in that dire circumstance." Today, I'm happy to report that my friend's husband is now resting comfortably at home and is expected to make a full recovery.

God appreciates a grateful heart. Throughout the day, offer God praise. If you see the awesome colors of an exquisite sunset, whisper, "Thank you, God." As your child's hand rests gently in yours, offer thanksgiving. When you're traveling and you get to your destination safely, utter a prayer of praise and thanks.

So praise God, even when life makes no sense at all. God will help you to "carry your cross," and give you peace. And at the midnight hour, as He did for Paul and Silas, His power could produce a miracle for you.

DAY FIVE:

GOD DWELLS IN HOMES FILLED WITH LOVE AND THANKFULNESS.

"Therefore, since we are surrounded by such a great cloud of witnesses, let us throw off everything that hinders and the sin that so easily entangles, and let us run with perseverance the race marked out for us."
HEBREWS 12:1, NIV

"Mommy, come here," said my daughter Sophia. I was returning e-mails in my home office, and I felt a gentle tug at my sleeve. So I stopped my typing, and with her little hand clasped in mine, I followed Sophia to the living room window.

It was early evening. We glanced up toward the heavens and, with certainty, she whispered, "Look, there's an angel, Mommy." I looked

The Biblical definition of an angel is "messenger." They carry out the commands of God. Protecting, guiding, angels are innumerable, and ascend and descend from heaven.

up and saw one lone, fluffy cloud situated right over our home, and it did appear to be in the shape of an angel.

I nodded my head, smiling at her in agreement, and my hand caressed her long, golden-brown ringlet curls. Then, with eyes of pure faith, Sophia joyfully declared, "Angels are around us!" At that moment, I recalled what the nineteenth-century British preacher Charles Spurgeon once wrote, "When home is ruled according to God's word, angels might be asked to stay with us, and they would not find themselves out of their element."

Our first memories are usually those of our homes. Children receive much of their schooling within the walls of their home, and their formation of character occurs largely under its roof. For, there, principles are taught, impressions are created, and personalities are developed.

A happy childhood is one of the best preparations for youngsters when they start on their own life's course. It is not the "house" that makes the home; it's the love, faith, and thankfulness within the house. For a home governed by these things is sure to be a happy home. "Now these three remain: faith, hope, and love. But the greatest of these is love" (1 Corinthians 13:13, NIV).

Look around at your surroundings and begin by asking yourself, "Am I leaving a legacy of love and thankfulness which my family will remember?" "How can I create lasting family memories?" "What can I do to give thanks and celebrate the blessings that God has given to me?"

An effective way is to promote family gatherings and create traditions to call your very own. Here is one of my favorite suggestions: Each day, be determined to have one family meal together and say grace.

Here's how: Join hands with those at your table. After that, take a moment of silence. Go around the table and have each person say their own special "grace." For saying grace is an excellent way to practice gratitude.

I've written some grace verses here to get you started:

- ✧ Grant us good health and friends to share our way. Keep us in your care, Lord, each precious day.

- ✧ God be with us as we walk each mile. Our life has a purpose and it is all worthwhile.

- ✧ Thank you for our food sent from God above. We accept it with His everlasting love.

- ✧ Thank you for this joyous day and for all the blessings that are coming our way.

- ✧ Bless our food and this home, we pray. May angels watch over us and keep us safe by night and day.

- ✧ God bless my family wherever they may be. Keep them safe, for they mean so much to me.

Mealtime can give you a chance to talk to one another and to enjoy uninterrupted time with your precious family. After you each say grace, you can also invite family members to take turns and share something good that happened that day, for which they are thankful. Gratitude is the greatest of virtues and the quickest access to the joy of life.

The evening meal has been hailed as one of the most important family gatherings. Research has suggested that the more often children eat dinner with their families, the less likely they are to smoke, drink, or use drugs.

"For each new morning with its light,
For rest and shelter of the night,
For health and food,
For love and friends,
For everything Thy goodness sends."

Ralph Waldo Emerson

So, back in my home office that evening, Sophia looked up at me with her beautiful little girl eyes and asked, "What should I be when I'm a big girl, Mommy?"

"You can be whatever you want to be, darling," I answered.

"I want to be good to people and love God," she replied.

President Lincoln said the same thing when he quoted the Old Testament Micah 6:8 (NKJV): "But to do justly, to love mercy, and to walk humbly with your God."

These timeless moments at home with my family are the essence of my life's delight in the gift that God has given me. In the Bible, God chose Abraham "to be the father of many nations" (Genesis 17:5) because He knew Abraham would "command His children and His household after Him, and they shall keep the way of the Lord, to do justice and judgment" (18:19).

Likewise, let's raise our children to love and honor God, for the possession of Godly character is to be valued far more than accomplishments, skills, or intelligence. Let us allow harmony, peace, and joy to be present in every room of our home, creating a Godly environment in all that we do:

✧ Pray together as a family.

✧ Read Bible verses and stories with one another.

✧ Encourage older children to have their own quiet "prayer and praise" time.

✧ Learn new praise songs, play musical instruments, and sing.

✧ Be truthful, respectful, and considerate of others.

"As for me and my house, we will serve the Lord."

Joshua 24:15

The lesson from Jesus's parable about the lost prodigal son, the boy who followed the wrong road to ruin before returning home to his father and finding redemption, tells us that if we have drifted away from God, we're always welcomed back with open arms.

Let the love and thankfulness that shines from your eyes be reflected in your home. God's angels will be encamped around you and will continuously be at your side. And you will live in the light of the open window.

DAY SIX:

IT'S TIME TO GIVE THANKS AND LIVE YOUR DREAM.

"Bless the Lord, O my soul, and forget none of His benefits;
Who pardons all your iniquities, Who heals all your diseases;
Who redeems your life from the pit, Who crowns you with
lovingkindness and compassion; Who satisfies your years with
good things, So that your youth is renewed like the eagle."

PSALM 103:2-5, NASB

There is a picturesque lake near our home, and when I pass by it and look out on the clear blue waters, I smile as I think of a story that I've heard about two friends who went fishing.

Early one day, the two friends, Mark and Bill, decided to go fishing at a lake across town. It was a beautiful, sun-filled morning and, equipped with their fishing rods and some bait, they planned to fish for the entire day in the pristine, open waters.

As the morning hours lengthened, one of the friends, Bill, carried out an odd fishing practice. When he would catch a fish, he would examine it closely. And, if the fish was really big, Bill would gently toss it back into the glistening lake.

All through the day, the two friends covered more and more

ground from their perch by the lake, and next they moved near to some large rocks to fish some more. Once again, if Bill reeled in a really large fish, he'd look at it, and then toss it back.

At one point, Bill cast his bait near a lily pad, and before long he caught another large fish. Yet again, Bill inspected the fish and tossed it back into the lake.

Many hours had passed, and Mark, having watched his friend curiously, sternly asked, "Bill, why are you throwing back into the lake all the really large fish that you catch?"

Quickly and matter-of-factly, Bill answered, "Well, I only have *a very small frying pan* in which to cook them."

Has something happened that has caused you to toss away your dreams and goals? Are you reluctant to dream really big dreams? Are you limiting yourself by your present situation? Do you think that the way your circumstance is now is the way it is always going to be?

We all face challenges and setbacks that initially seem to be insurmountable. And then, because of these unforeseen problems, similar to Bill who tossed back into the lake all the "big fish" that he caught, we too, may toss back our big dreams, big goals, and big plans for our future.

Today, allow yourself to imagine the life that you desire, and give thanks that you can live your dream!

Five years from now, if there were no obstacles in your path, what big dreams would you have implemented? If your potential were unlimited, what kind of life would you create for yourself and your family?

The key is to first dream big, God-sized dreams, think big thoughts, and create a clear mental picture of where you are going, for we tend to travel in the direction of our dominant thoughts. Then, with faith, call those big dreams forth, as if they were *already* here, and work toward them.

> *"You pay God a compliment by*
> *asking great things of Him."*
>
> —Saint Teresa of Avila

In the Bible, Abraham was a great role model of faith. Even when there was nothing left to dream or hope for, Abraham still hoped and believed. "Why?" you may ask. Because his trust was not in human capabilities, it was in the divine power of God. Abraham was called the "father of all who believe" (Romans 4:11, NIV). We need his sort of steadfast faith to safeguard us when we are pursuing our big, God-sized dreams.

Perhaps, fears have threatened to pull you down. Maybe you received some discouraging news. Or else, someone might have intentionally tried to hurt you. And at this point, you're worn out and tired, saying, "It's just not worth it anymore."

But, keep in mind that God wants to bless you. He wants to give you the desires of your heart. He wants you to succeed. Therefore, don't settle and toss away your precious dreams. Your thoughts create your reality, so offer prayers of gratitude for your God-given abilities, and choose to live your dream.

Take the challenge:

✧ Live as you want to be remembered. This is one method for deciding how to live fully. Ask yourself today, "How do I want my family and friends to remember me? How do I want to be remembered in the world?"

✧ Once you have your answer, start now by making those characteristics and aspirations tangible.

✧ Always give thanks. Gratitude is the energy that fuels the manifestations of your desires.

✧ Be grateful for the gift of your precious life. For the world is a better place because you dared to live your dream.

Years ago, I read a story somewhere about a boy nicknamed "Sparky." In his youth, he must have felt like an underdog, as it was said that Sparky was a shy and awkward boy. But God had given him a gift—the ability to draw—and Sparky was thankful for that talent. "Someday, you're going to be an artist," a kindergarten teacher once said to him. And he held that dream in his heart.

Yet, Sparky was rejected over and over. In his senior year of high school, he submitted some drawings to the editors of his yearbook. He was turned down, and this was painful. Sparky also sent some art samples to various companies. Yet, he was rejected time and again.

Sparky worked at various odd jobs, and was in the service, but never settled for average, being thankful for his dream and not letting it go. Eventually, a creative idea came to Sparky: he decided to draw his autobiography in a comic strip. The hurts of his early years provided the material, as he described his childhood in pictures: a little boy who was an underachiever, a child who was not popular and who was clumsy. He drew pictures of himself holding a kite that would never fly, kicking a football and falling down, and losing a baseball game.

So, Sparky the cartoon, based on Sparky the boy, who was shy and rejected, became the famous cartoon character Charlie Brown in his comic strip *Peanuts!* Every time Charles Schulz failed, he bounced back. Schulz never gave up on God's good plan for his life. He dreamed a big dream and made it come true! You can do the same.

Start by asking yourself: "What do I want to accomplish?" "How do I want to use my gifts?" If some doors have shut on you, find the courage to keep searching for an open window. Choose to believe, and say with a nod, "It's possible," and utter a word of thanks, for with God, all things are possible.

"There are loyal hearts; there are spirits brave; there are souls that are pure and true. Then give the world the best you have. And the best will come back to you."

MADELINE BRIDGES

I believe in your great potential. You were created by God to influence others for His glory and for their good. So, be thankful that you can dream God-sized dreams, and now go out and make all of them come true!

DAY SEVEN:

STEP INTO THE FULLNESS OF YOUR DESTINY.

*"The Lord is good to all: and His tender mercies
are over all His works."*

PSALM 145:9

One evening, at the dinner table, my imaginative daughter Sophia looked at me from across the table and casually asked, "Mommy, what do you want to be when you grow up . . . a butterfly or a flower?"

Smiling at such a question coming from my little curly-haired girl, I answered, "I want to be a flower." Continuing the conversation, she inquired, "What color flower do you want to be . . . a white flower or a purple flower?" I responded quickly, "I'll be a white flower." Satisfied with my answer, she picked up her fork and resumed eating her macaroni.

What do you want to be? Who are you? Moreover, *Who will you be?*

For weeks after this conversation with my sweet daughter, I have been asking myself those same questions. Today, I'd like you to ask yourself them, too.

Many times, we set out enthusiastically for a life full of joy and purpose. We want to make the world a better place; we try to improve ourselves, to make our dreams a reality, and fulfill our calling. And what happens? Life throws us a curveball. We may make an attempt for a goal, but we hit a brick wall. Out of nowhere, someone purposely tries to push us down, and maybe we make a wrong choice, leading us to a dead end. In our pillows we cry, "Are my dreams over?" "Where do I belong?" "Is life over for me now?"

We may feel defined by our careers, our spouses, our looks or status; but then if we lose any of them, we ourselves can be off-course—feeling devalued, unraveled. But *who you are* and *who you will be* has nothing to do with another person, your credentials, appearance, or position. Your great worth comes from being a child of God. Affirm each day, "I love and approve of myself exactly the way God created me."

"We can easily forgive a child who is afraid of the dark; the real tragedy of life is when men are afraid of the light."

PLATO

You are a special creation of God's love and your life has profound meaning. You are one in a million and your worth, to God, is far greater than the brightest star in the sky or ten thousand worlds. No matter the circumstance, regardless of what stage of life you are in, despite past struggles, God is not finished with the divine plan He has for you yet.

Now, I'd like you to get in touch with the child within. Keep some framed childhood photographs of yourself in your home and office, places where you can view the pictures often. Let the childhood photos remind you, "who you really are"—your authenticity, goodness, and fervor for life.

I know a businesswoman, Melanie, who lost a long-standing, prestigious career. Months had passed and she just couldn't get over the loss, for she equated her self-worth with her business achievements.

One day, a dear friend of hers sent her a card that read, "You are a good person . . . who knows where God will lead you—just be secure in the fact that He will lead you in the right direction. All is well as long as you have faith in Him."

As Melanie read her friend's words, they brought clarity to her, thus allowing her to begin to regain her sense of worth and move on. Melanie realized that *who she was* had nothing to do with externals. She was a child of God, she had great attributes, and He still had wonderful goals within her grasp.

> *"At times our own light goes out and is rekindled*
> *by a spark from another person. Each of us*
> *has cause to think with deep gratitude of those*
> *who have lighted the flame within us."*
>
> ALBERT SCHWEITZER

Send thank you notes to people who may need encouragement or have had a profound impact on your life. Expressing thankfulness in your note and paying tribute to them is powerful. Moreover, the thank you note can also be saved, re-read, and treasured, creating a joy that can continue on.

Please take a moment and put in writing five favorite traits about yourself, and thank God for those qualities. Slip the piece of paper in your day planner or wallet to look at it whenever you need a little lift.

You are braver, stronger, and smarter than you think. Designed in the awesome mind of God, you are the most beloved of all of His creations. Ephesians 1:4 (NKJV) says, " . . . He chose us in Him before the foundation of the world, that we should be holy and without blame before Him in love." Within you there are qualities that you have not yet discovered, unlimited abilities and talents. Make the most of "what you are." Do you possess qualities such as patience, dependability, or a great disposition? Celebrate them! Are you an understanding friend, a good neighbor, or an animal lover? Honor that!

Bear in mind, you can't change the past, but you can leave it behind so you can go forward. Have you learned anything positive from your past experiences? Use your past as a learning tool. Let go of guilt, regrets, bitterness, and negativity. See what went wrong and make the necessary changes now, so that your future becomes a bright and welcoming place. Tip: If negative thoughts start to speed out of control, call a trusted friend and talk it through. After that, don't discuss the issue again.

Copy this quote, post it where you can view it, and read it daily: "What lies behind us and what lies before us are small matters compared to what lies within us. And when we bring what is within us out into the world, miracles happen."

RALPH WALDO EMERSON

I want you to be at peace, and rest in who God made you to be. Always be honest and authentic. God loves and esteems you.

So, hold on to your values and do not compromise them. Persist in being good to people, spreading joy to others. There is no limit to what you can accomplish for the good of mankind.

Going back to the Bible, in John 17:4, Jesus and His disciples were approaching the Garden of Gethsemane. Jesus was sorrowful over His impending death. First, He was teaching His disciples, and next, He was praying His great prayer to the Father, uttering, "I have brought you glory on earth by completing the work you gave me to do" (NIV). To bring glory to God should be our ultimate goal, as well.

Today is a new day and with it comes a clean slate. Therefore, delight in the newness of the pristine morning, wake up, and say, "Thank you, Lord. A new chapter begins today and it is only the start of bringing you glory and expecting wonderful things for my future."

Take time to be alone, still, and quiet, to listen to the echoes of your heart. What is it telling you?

As our journey together draws to a close, I'd like you to ask yourself these two last questions, "What have I discovered about myself up to this point?" and "How can I apply what I've learned to the rest of my life?" Write down the answers.

My mind wanders back to my daughter's question, "What do you want to be when you grow up?" And I recognize what matters most in life is who we are, how much joy we give out to others, and how much love and peace is in our hearts.

And so, my dear readers, my wish is for you to "step into the fullness of your destiny" and let God guide you to be the best you can be.

AFTERWORD

"Do all to the glory of God."

1 CORINTHIANS 10:31

It is a late summer afternoon, and I am sitting on a lounge chair at the beach, with my three daughters playing in the sand in front of me. I've almost completed writing this book, and tears of gratitude fill my eyes. Throughout these eight chapters, I have gone through a transformation, developing a peace and a trust in God like none I've experienced before. So, prior to us parting for a time, let me share with you one last story.

Once, there was an 18-year-old lad who wanted to leave his family's country farm where he was raised, to venture out on his own to the big city. After some time, the lad's father agreed to allow his son to go forth alone.

The father took the lad to the train station and hugged him good-bye and then, suitcase in hand, the youngster boarded the train. At first, the lad felt bold and excited to see the world. Yet, never having been away from the comforts of home and not knowing anyone in the big city, he soon became frightened.

As the lad sat by himself on the train, the conductor came by. He was particularly friendly to the young lad, and talked with him for a long time, giving him advice on where to go and how to get around in the city. Then, a kindly, smiling woman approached the lad. She offered him some food to eat, and since she lived in the city, she also gave him her address in case he needed anything. Next, a businessman approached him and told him that when they reached their destination, he'd walk with him and help him to find a nice place to stay and, possibly, lend a hand in securing him a job.

Months later, the lad learned a secret: His father had ridden the train to the city with him, sitting unseen in a seat in the back while devotedly sending people to help his beloved son.

You are a much-loved daughter or son of God. And all along life's path, just as the lad's father had sent people to assist his son, your heavenly Father will send people to help you. And I hope that through these pages, I have been that person whom God extended his help through to assist you on your journey.

Dear reader, trust in God's faithfulness, as He is holding out His loving arms to you. For one day you will see that all of your heart's dreams have finally come together. And what you have prayed for and always wished for has finally and delightfully come to pass.

God has something wonderful for you . . . the blessing is within your reach—it's just a matter of time and you will see the Open Window.

Until we meet again, God bless you *always,*
Catherine

ABOUT THE AUTHOR

Catherine Galasso-Vigorito's nationally syndicated weekly newspaper column has endeared her to readers nationwide for over seventeen years.

Known for her ability to uplift and encourage, Catherine has become America's most beloved inspirational voice, inspiring people toward a better life.

Catherine is a bestselling author and also writes a monthly column of encouragement for our servicemen and women that is distributed both in the States and overseas.

In addition, Catherine has designed inspirational products that carry her messages of hope in gift stores and online, and she appears live on QVC Television, bringing her product line to people from all walks of life.

Catherine held the Miss Connecticut U.S.A. title, and worked for twelve years for Clear Channel Radio. She appears frequently on television, hosting, reporting, and offering inspirational commentary.

Catherine lives on the East Coast with her husband, their three daughters, and many pets. You can visit her website at www.anewyouworldwide.com